T5-CGB-834

Special Friends

TWILA KNAACK

Special Friends

WHO REFLECT
THE FRUIT OF THE SPIRIT

WORD BOOKS
PUBLISHER
WACO, TEXAS

SPECIAL FRIENDS
Copyright © 1981 by Word Incorporated.
All rights reserved. No part of this book may be reproduced in any form, except for brief quotations in reviews, without the written permission of the publisher.

ISBN 0-8499-2901-6
Library of Congress Cat. Card No: 80-54555
Printed in the United States of America

Ruth Graham's poem on pp. 17–18 is from *Sitting By My Laughing Fire,* copyright © 1977 by Ruth Bell Graham, and is used by permission of Word Books, Publisher, Waco, Texas 76796.

The hymn, "It Is Well With My Soul" (p. 41), copyright 1918 John Church Company, is used by permission of the publisher.

The Song, "I Could Never Outlove the Lord," (p. 82) by William J. and Gloria Gaither is © copyright 1972 by William J. Gaither. All rights reserved. Used by permission of The Benson Company, Inc., Nashville.

To my parents
NORA AND MELVIN KNAACK
whose everyday lives
taught me
the fruit of the Spirit

THANKS TO . . .

Joan and Bill Brown—for their constant encouragement and their faith in me that I could write a book.

Nancy Moyer, Janice Barfield and Anita Beal—for their continual interest when my interest seemed to wane.

Carol Anderson, Lynn Gescheider, and Tessie Que—my prayer partners who constantly uplifted me in the project.

The fruit of the Spirit is love,
joy, peace, patience, kindness, goodness,
faithfulness, gentleness, self-control.
—Galatians 5:22–23

CONTENTS

INTRODUCTION

A farmer went to a State Fair and proudly boasted, "I have a farm I want to enter into the competition. It's bound to win a prize because there's not a single weed on it. There's not a bit of poison oak, no hint of thistles, not a trace of mullein. Absolutely, positively no weeds."

"Well," said the registrar at the fair, "what are your crops?"

"Oh, well, I . . . um . . . I . . ." stammered the farmer. "I haven't produced any crops. But there's not a single weed."

What a lesson. God doesn't have any use for a nonproductive Christian. It is by our fruits that we verify our love for him.

Paul, in his Epistle to the Galatians, writes frankly about the products of the flesh, but he doesn't stop at listing the "weeds." He goes on to list for the Galatians the new characteristics the Holy Spirit will gradually produce in their lives: "But the fruit of the Spirit is love, joy, peace, patience, kindness, goodness, faithfulness, gentleness, self-control; against such things there is no law" (Gal. 5:22–23, NAS).

What a need our world has for such fruit! Everywhere people are looking for love, longing for peace, experiencing to find joy. Headlines tell of crisis after crisis which threatens to plunge the world into chaos. Millions seek frantically for something to give happiness and peace of mind. The simple answer is in the words Jesus spoke: "I am come that you might have life and have it more abundantly."

Our lives are truly abundant when the fruit of the Spirit is evident. Friends get an uplift being around us; husbands look forward to coming home after a tiring day at the office; children are more prone to obey. Think of the influence we can have with each person with whom we come in contact—the grocer, the saleslady, the neighbor, the friend at church. A gentle word, a smile of kindness, love that doesn't hold a grudge—that kind of fruitful living can brighten someone's day, or even change another's life.

As a matter of fact, that is one reason the Holy Spirit grows fruit in our lives. Spiritual fruit is not only for our own needs; our lives bear fruit so that we might be able to share it with others. When non-Christian friends see the fruit of the Spirit, they will no doubt be aware that something is missing from their lives, and be more open to the message of Christ.

How does the fruit of the Spirit grow in our lives? My research for this book has shown me that the nine characteristics listed in Galatians come as an intact package. The word *fruit* is singular. We're not to pick out one aspect and cultivate it—the Holy Spirit wants to produce *all nine* in our lives.

A lot has been said about love, peace, and joy, the "reaching up" or "Godward" aspects of spiritual fruit. In my study, I found I had to do a little more digging to understand the "humanward" or "reaching out" aspects—patience, kindness, and goodness. The last three fruit are "selfward" or "reaching in"—faithfulness, meaning dependability; gentleness, also translated as meekness and denoting a mild manner; and self-control, which means temperance in all things.

It is important that we see the difference between words or ideas and real fruit. Natural fruit cannot be manufactured by a machine; it must grow on trees. Spiritual fruit also must grow naturally, out of a life controlled and directed by the Holy Spirit.

When we have the right attitude-fruit, then we can produce action-fruit. My pastor, John MacArthur, gave this example in one of his sermons: "Imagine you are in an orchard. There's this fellow up in a tree picking fruit, and you are down below with a basket. The guy in the tree yells down, 'Hey, I'm going to be dropping some apples, so you take your basket and catch them.' The fruit starts coming down, but if you have your basket upside down and you're not paying attention, it will be dropping all around you. All you have to do is get your basket in the right spot, right side up, and the apples will go right in. It's that way in the Christian life. God's Holy Spirit keeps producing; receiving is only a question of where your basket is. Developing the fruit of the Spirit is a matter of submitting yourself to the productivity of the Holy Spirit."

The climate must be right before natural fruit can grow. So it is with the spiritual fruit in our lives. It grows gradually, nurtured by the study of God's word. We can't expect a full crop overnight. And fruit doesn't grow without effort; it takes ceaseless vigilance and a constant struggle to be all Christ wants us to be. Richard Halverson once said, "Growing in grace and in the knowledge of Jesus Christ works this way. . . . The school of the Spirit involves suffering, pain, failure, sin, . . . all of which are recycled by the grace of God into maturity."

At the same time, the making of a Christlike character

doesn't depend on our inexhaustible enthusiasm, but is accomplished by the Holy Spirit in us. When the battle gets too difficult, and the situation uncontrollable, Christ will reenforce us. Napoleon, patrolling his camp during the war, discovered a sentry sound asleep. He gently took the musket out of the man's hand and marched up and down until dawn. The soldier awoke to find his general keeping watch.

A lot has been said and written about the fruit of the Spirit, and all Christians can profit by using such resources to enrich their understanding. But as we grow into full maturity we often need more than books—we need examples to follow.

That is my real purpose in writing this *Special Friends.* The growing of the fruit of the Spirit is done by God, but he has used nine godly women who possess the complete package of spiritual fruit to be examples to me. These women, whom I count as my friends, have inspired me, taught me, and made me stretch my own thinking. I want to pass on to you the valuable lessons I have learned from these women of God, in the hope that you will begin today to let the Holy Spirit bring forth fruit in your life.

Ruth Bell Graham

LOVE

The fruit of the Spirit is LOVE. . . .

Ruth Bell Graham

"What the world needs now is love, sweet love," the song goes. "No, not just for some, but for everyone." Odd that even those who do not know the love of God somehow sense that love is the basic answer to all human ills. Indeed, someone aptly said, "Love is the doorway through which the human soul passes from selfishness to service and from solitude to kinship with all mankind." All other bridges from one soul to another crumble under the stress of time and circumstances. Only love has the strength to wait; to be kind and generous; to be humbly unselfish; to be courteous, guileless, sincere, and of an even temper. Only love can suffer all things, believe all things, and go on hoping. Love alone never fails. So teaches the Bible, and so is proven in the arena of human experience.

Even Napoleon is reported to have said, "Alexander, Caesar, Charlemagne and myself founded empires on force, and they perished. Jesus of Nazareth alone founded his Kingdom on love, and at this hour millions of men are ready to die for him."

Someone once described love as "the tickle in your heart which you cannot scratch." Love is intangible, but it can be easily recognized by its characteristics. Love embraces the qualities we all long for—those described in Paul's letter to the Corinthians: "Love is patient, love is kind, and is not jealous; love does not brag and is not arrogant, does not act unbecomingly; it does not seek its own, is not provoked, does not take into account a wrong suffered, does not rejoice in unrighteousness, but rejoices with the truth; bears all things, believes all things, hopes all things, endures all things. Love never fails" (1 Cor. 13:4–8).

But where does love begin? Where all things began . . . in God. Love shows itself in his love for his creation. The closest glimpse we get of such love is when we enter the process of creation ourselves—when a child is born. The love a mother and father have for their child is the simplest and clearest portrayal of love on the human scale. This love is so basic to our needs that a child who grows up deprived of love often suffers psychological damage no medical treatment can ever correct. Faced with growing numbers of women who rebel against staying in the home, even secular psychologists warn of the dangers of leaving the rearing of children to institutions. Tiny infants die for lack of love, children suffer, and adults disintegrate under the pain of being unloved.

The theme of love permeates the Bible. In the Song of Solomon, that beautiful canticle of love, the bridegroom sings, "Set me as a seal upon thine heart, as a seal upon thine arm: for love is strong as death . . ." (Song of Sol. 8:6, KJV).

A very clear picture of love's compelling power is given in the book of Hebrews: "Looking unto Jesus the author and finisher of our faith; who for the joy that was set before him endured the cross, despising the shame, and is set down at the right hand of the throne of God" (12:2, KJV). What is the joy that was set before Jesus? What did he have after his ascension that he did not have before he took on human flesh? Us . . . you and me . . . the redemption of all mankind. Is this not love?

God loved us so much, he gave his Son, and ever since that first advent love has been defined in terms of giving. What more could Jesus have done to convince us of his overwhelming love? Nothing! The Cross was the ultimate evidence.

Under the shower of God's love for us as individuals, love ceases to be just something we feel; it is something we share. A life yielded to Christ can see love's power bring transformation. And then it will spill over on to others. Amy Carmichael summed it up when she said, "You can give without loving but you can't love without giving."

This fact of faith was lived out before Ruth Bell all through her childhood. Born in China of missionary parents, Ruth grew up knowing she was loved, not only by her parents, but most of all by her heavenly Father. From a rich spiritual background, Ruth came through the throes of doubt to a mature, committed faith in Jesus Christ. This heritage of love and faith was important to her when she became Mrs. Billy Graham in 1943.

Prior to meeting Billy, Ruth's desire was to return to China as an unmarried missionary. But on their first date Ruth realized she'd met the kind of man she'd like to marry. She had prayed for a godly man before she met the tall, lanky student at Wheaton, and that prayer had been expressed in a poem she wrote:

> Dear God, I prayed, all unafraid
> (as we're inclined to do)
> I do not need a handsome man
> but let him be like You;

I do not need one big and strong
nor yet so very tall,
nor need he be some genius,
or wealthy, Lord, at all;
but let his head be high, dear God,
and let his eye be clear,
his shoulders straight, whate'er his state,
whate'er his earthly sphere;
and let his face have character,
a ruggedness of soul,
and let his whole life show, dear God,
a singleness of goal;
then when he comes
(as he will come)
with quiet eyes aglow,
I'll understand that he's the man
I prayed for long ago.

Though the determination she showed at first to go to the mission field nearly broke up her romance (he argued long and convincingly), Ruth eventually accepted the fact that God's first calling for her was to be Billy's wife. She once said, "God never asks us to give up one thing without giving so much in return that you wind up almost ashamed of yourself."

For Mrs. Graham, biblical principles, bathed in love, have set the course of her decision making. Though she could have traveled the world with her husband or made a career for herself, she chose to remain at home in North Carolina to rear their five children. She has, in so choosing, fulfilled the injunction found in Titus 2:4–5: "That they may teach the young women to be sober, to love their husbands, to love their children, to be discreet, chaste, keepers at home, good, obedient to their own husbands, that the word of God be not blasphemed" (KJV).

Her decision to "keep at home" while their children were young often meant lonely times for the young Mrs. Graham. When he was away preaching during the early years of their marriage, "I missed him so much that I remember sleeping with his sports coat for company." But, she says, "It was never indifference to each other or lack of love that caused us to live such separate lives. We made a commitment to the Lord and followed the Lord's leading. In response to that, he gave us extra love for one another and extra understanding. It wasn't easy, but Christ never promised it would be."

At home in North Carolina, Ruth Graham translated her love into her world. How? By being there . . . not only to wash the clothes and scrub the floors and prepare the meals, but to listen, to touch, to laugh, to kiss away tears and settle arguments.

Disciplining the children was a job that fell largely on Ruth over the years. When asked if she ever spanked the children, she laughs as she says, "Heavens, yes!"

Though Ruth was strict with the children, she was gentle as she taught them to think of God very simply as a heavenly Father who cares for them very much. Early in their lives she taught them to pray. "I think that spontaneous prayers are best for small children," Ruth says. "Just 'God bless Mama and Daddy,' and right down the line, winding up with 'I love you.' I'm not sure how much they understand, but they're getting the idea that they're talking to someone who loves them and cares about them."

Next to the Bible, Ruth has often recommended, *A Parent's Guide to the Emotional Needs of Children,* by Dr. David Goodman (NY: Hawthorn Books, 1969), as perhaps the finest book she's read on child rearing. "He says the best thing two parents can do for their children is to love and appreciate each other, and then to love and appreciate the child. Some parents don't let their children know that they are loved and appreciated. It's so important to express it— not 'I like you if you please me,' but 'I like you just the way you are.' "

With their father away for months on end while they were growing up, the Graham children naturally missed him. Yet, even though he was often not there when they needed him, they remember their childhood as being dominated by the enjoyment of his presence rather than by resentment of his absence. The children, now all grown and married, attribute this to the sterling character of their mother. They themselves tell it best:

Franklin: "It did not matter who our parents were with, or where they were. If I wanted to talk, they were always ready to stop and listen. . . . My mother was always bright and sparkly, even when she worried herself sick over some problem, or when she would only get an hour or two of sleep at night. She might have been worrying about some student at college or some member of her Sunday School class or me—like when I was growing up and wouldn't get home until four o'clock in the morning. Mother never went to bed until all of us children were in. She has that bright, cheerful personality, and I believe it comes from her daily walk with the Lord."

Anne: "Our parents set the tone for our lives by the way they lived theirs. Their depending on God was obvious—they loved the Lord, and they shared that love with me. Mother's light would be on late at night and early in the morning as she studied her Bible and prayed. At the age of three, on Mother's knee, I asked the Lord Jesus to come into my heart."

Gigi: "When Daddy was able to be there, he was always loving and affectionate with each of us. But mother was always there. We did everything together as friends and companions.

"I saw Daddy live what he preached. I saw them making Christ their life, not just their religion.

"I was always secure in love, and I knew that whatever I did I would always, always be loved. Oh, it was often tough love, and never cheap sympathy, but my parents made it very clear that they would always love me, even if they didn't love what I did. My parents taught us from the very beginning that this type of love is the same as God's love for us. He loves a sinner, but hates the sin."

Bunny: "Mother made it a point to make Daddy's homecoming special. She talked about it for days ahead; it was something to look forward to. They were very affectionate . . . . we were always aware that they were in love with each other."

Ned: "My home has always been a warm place. It has always meant security. Mother has always offered so much love. She always enjoys learning about something new.

"Ruth's ministry has always seemed to be to individuals—in her home or outside. While her husband speaks to thousands, Ruth is called time and again to speak to one . . . one lost . . . one forgotten."

As I was working at a crusade in Las Vegas, I watched Ruth minister to a young distressed girl. A major story had appeared in the local newspaper, telling of the girl's attempt to cut off her hand after misinterpreting Matthew 5:30: "If thy right hand offend thee, cut it off . . ." (KJV). Ruth made frequent visits to the hospital to counsel the girl, to touch her with love.

At that same crusade, a hippie-type fellow came into the office wanting to speak to Billy Graham. He was told Billy was not there, but instead was introduced to Ruth.

While others went on drinking coffee and chatting, Ruth found a quiet corner where they could talk. With her worn Bible, full of underlined verses and notations in the margins, she patiently and lovingly told the shabbily dressed man of Christ's love. When the young man comprehended what Christ did at Calvary, the two knelt in prayer as the man confessed his sin.

Joan Winmill Brown is another one who has felt Ruth's tender concern for individuals. Ruth was with her husband at his 1954 crusade in London. After the message, when the throngs of converts had been ushered to rooms for counsel, the two women met—Joan, whose spirit had just awakened to the love of God in Christ, and Ruth, who knew him well.

Joan remembers, "Her face had an openness of expression. My first thoughts were, 'What a truly beautiful woman! She has such an aura of serenity.' . . . How I longed for this!" Ruth read to Joan from her Bible, and reassured her of Christ's abiding presence in her life. Then, like an old friend, Ruth ushered Joan to a small dressing room to meet her husband. Joan was amazed to learn her counselor that night was Mrs. Billy Graham! And that evening was not the end. Ruth kept contact with Joan and made moves to build a lasting friendship . . . a book sent, an invitation to tea, correspondence. Little things, but acts of love that were God's tools in the early reshaping of Joan's life.

Love looks for ways to be constructive, to serve and to be available, and Ruth Graham has shown that kind of love over and over. A Cambodian family, with very few belongings and a very meager knowledge of the English language moved into Ruth's tiny town of Montreat, North Carolina. A well-meaning lady gave the little Cambodian girl a stuffed frog to play with, but the child was terribly frightened of it and threw it in a closet.

When Ruth learned the effect the American toy had on the Oriental girl, she rummaged through a trunk in her attic until she found a little Chinese doll she had played with as a child. She took this doll to the little Cambodian girl. When the child recognized the Chinese face on the doll, her eyes widened, and she tightly clutched her new toy.

Over and over again in the Scriptures, Jesus said, "If you love me, keep my commandments" (John 14:15, KJV). What commandments? "A new commandment I give unto you, That ye love one another" (John 13:34, KJV) and "Go ye into all the world, and preach the gospel to every creature" (Mark 16:15, KJV).

In love for Jesus Christ, Billy Graham has gone into all the world preaching, and thousands have come to know the Lord. And in love and obedience to Jesus Christ, Ruth Graham has filled her world with love. It is a smaller world, perhaps, than her husband's . . . for years populated mostly by five pairs of busy little feet. But to Ruth has come the wonder of seeing her children born in the Spirit, and the joy of a strong, fulfilling marriage.

Billy Graham says, "I believe that marriage can be built on the spiritual level, and that it provides . . . spiritual ties. Our love has deepened because it is built on the right foundation. We have never been unhappy one day since our marriage. We know with certainty that we were God's choice for each other."

For Ruth Graham, certainly, has the Scripture come true: "Her children arise up, and call her blessed; her husband also, and he praiseth her" (Prov. 31:28, KJV).

Kathie Lee Johnson

JOY

The fruit of the Spirit is love, JOY. . . .

Kathie Lee Johnson

The air conditioner goes out the day the temperature tips the 110-degree mark, the drains back up, huge car-repair bills arrive in the morning's mail. And the Apostle Paul has the nerve to say "Rejoice evermore" (1 Thess. 5:17, KJV)?

It is easy to confuse happiness with joy. Happiness is produced by external circumstances; it can quickly disappear when someone bursts our bubble with an unkind word or deed. Joy comes from deep within, and no one can take it away. John 16:22 says, "You will rejoice; . . . and no one can rob you of that joy" (TLB).

It's pretty hard to show happiness when a tooth aches or when a friend's death leaves a void in our lives, but even in such experiences we can know the joy of the Lord.

Christ never promised us a rose garden without thorns. In fact, God allows the elements of joy and pain to be mixed. James 1:2 says, "Consider it all joy . . . when you encounter various trials." We often desire to experience a life that bypasses sorrow or suffering. But God's ultimate plan is for us to reach his goals, even though the road we travel may be both smooth and rough.

The British flag flies over Buckingham palace to signify when the Queen is in residence. Joy should be the standard that identifies us as Christians and indicates that the King of Kings resides within our hearts. Our joy should be so obvious to those around us that it is contagious. The face of the Christian should glow, to contrast sharply with the faces of despairing people who don't know Christ. "A joyful heart makes a cheerful face," Solomon wrote in Proverbs 15:13. Complete joy is a twenty-four-hour-a-day experience. Our zest for life should be evident from our waking moment on!

Joy is a positive approach to life, one that springs from unselfishness. We are what we think we are; that's why Paul said, "Whatever is true, whatever is honorable, whatever is right, whatever is pure, whatever is lovely, whatever is of good repute, if there is any excellence and if anything worthy of praise, let your mind dwell on these things" (Phil. 4:8).

A. B. Simpson explains how the fullness of the Spirit must crowd out our pain, doubt, fear, and sorrow, and must bring the joy of Christ to fill our beings: "What is it that makes the melody in an organ? It is not only the touch of skillful fingers on the keys, but it is the filling of the pipes by the movement of the pedals. I may have the ability to play the most skillful tunes, but unless the organ is filled, I try in vain. Likewise, our songs of praise are dead and cold until the breath of God fills all the channels of our being. Then comes the heart-song of praise and the overflowing fountain of gladness."

An old Chinese proverb says "One joy dispels a hundred cares." Laughter can turn the most frustrating moment into a joyful occasion. Proverbs 17:22 says, "A cheerful heart does good like medicine" (TLB).

God wants to so permeate our lives with joy that, even

when it spills over to others, the Holy Spirit continues to keep us full to the brim. John 15:11 says, "These things I have spoken to you, that My joy may be in you, and that your joy may be made full." If our joy is "full," we will have that inward peace that cannot be affected by outward circumstances.

David, in learning to praise God, found that God's "anger is but for a moment,/His favor is for a lifetime;/Weeping may last for the night,/But a shout of joy comes in the morning" Psalms 30:5.

The Holy Spirit is at work in us "both to will and to work for His good pleasure" (Phil. 2:13), producing joy in our lives.

Too often we go about routinely doing our work, and reserve our joy for special occasions. But life can seem so unexciting if we keep on thinking, "I'll save up more time when the kids are grown, and then I'll have time to be happy." Christ wants us to have joy *now!*

A result of Christian joy is expressed in Ephesians 5:19: "Speaking to one another in psalms and hymns and spiritual songs, singing and making melody with your heart to the Lord."

That verse is a good description of Kathie Lee Johnson. With unbounding exuberance, this talented girl faces life head on, sharing her love for Jesus Christ and using her God-given talent to sing his praises. "Something happens inside of me that creates joy, the more I sing gospel music and songs that deal with the triumph of the Christian life," Kathie told me from her home in Woodland Hills, California.

Music has always played an important role in Kathie's life, and she credits her parents with instilling in her an appreciation for all types of music. The brown-eyed, brown-haired singer remembers when she and Michie, a younger sister, would pretend to hold microphones and sing their hearts out as they dazzled an imaginary audience.

Kathie's zest for living and boundless enthusiasm is a basic part of her personality. However, at age eleven, she found the *eternal* joy only Christ gives when she committed her life to him at a showing of Billy Graham's film, *The Restless Ones.* "That night I asked the Lord to make something beautiful out of my life. That's part of the abundant joy I now have," the ever-bubbling Kathie says.

Being reared in a Christian family made it only natural for Kathie to begin her singing career in the church. Her duets with Michie were an often-requested part of the church services. It soon became evident Michie had the natural talent in the family. However, when a voice teacher told Kathie, "stick to harmony," the youngster only became more determined to prove to the world she could be a soloist. After three months of practicing, the zealous teenager won the talent award that helped her gain the title of Junior Miss in her hometown of Bowie, Maryland.

There was no stopping the determined gal as she went on to win the state title and represented Maryland in the national finals at Mobile, Alabama, where her talent entry consisted of singing a spiritual. She went home from the pageant with a fifteen-hundred-dollar scholarship and a contract to film a commercial for Kraft, one of the sponsors of the event.

To further develop and use her talent for singing, Kathie enrolled at Oral Roberts University and became a member of the World Action Singers. This brought her to Hollywood for the recording and taping of Mr. Roberts's TV specials. Kathie's motto became, "Don't fill your life with years; fill your years with life," as she acquainted herself with show business and those involved in it.

In 1975, with limited experience but with a burning desire to work as an entertainer, Kathie moved to Hollywood to search for work.

Dick Ross, who had produced the Oral Roberts television shows, remembers when the effervescent Kathie bounced into his Hollywood office at NBC and announced she had come to get a job in television. He says, "Knowing she was coming to the most difficult place to get a job because of so much stiff competition, I simply wished her good luck. I figured the next time I would hear from Kathie, she would be back in Maryland. That same afternoon, the grinning Kathie came back into my office to say, 'Well, I'll be seeing a lot more of you, because I just got a job on "Days of Our Lives" [a popular daytime drama].' But the more I thought about it, I wasn't surprised. When Kathie goes after something, it is the immovable object being moved by the irresistible force."

To Kathie, being joyful means "flowing" in God's will. "I'm never really happy when I'm still. The challenge and adventure come in trusting him and moving out. If we step out with him, knowing that 'greater is he that is in us than he that is in the world,' then we don't have to be afraid we'll fail or be rejected. My joy comes from looking in the background of my life—seeing what God has already done and coupling it with his promises. The excitement of what he is going to do makes each new day thrilling. Nehemiah 8:10 says, 'The joy of the Lord is your strength' (KJV). Unless I have that joy, I don't have the ability to step out, to dare to live the Christian life," Kathie admits.

During one of Kathie's Hollywood visits as a college student, she met Paul Johnson, a young gospel-music composer and arranger. Having admired his work for several years, she found him to be as appealing as his music. Upon moving to Hollywood, she began attending a Bible study in his home, and their relationship began to deepen. In April, 1976, they were married.

Soon after she became Mrs. Paul Johnson, Kathie relinquished her acting on "Days of Our Lives" in order to devote her full time to being a housewife. Her efforts to be the perfect wife programed her to regularly have a candlelight dinner on the table when her handsome, blue-eyed husband arrived home from work. However, the sparkle began to diminish from the new bride. "I found myself crying a lot for no real reason," Kathie confesses, "and I felt Paul wasn't as thrilled with me as I hoped he would be. We came to the conclusion that I was not all that fascinating when I stayed home and did the cleaning and cooking. Paul wanted me to be my own person as well as his companion." Kathie remembers Paul once telling her, "Don't make me responsible for all your happiness. I don't want that responsibility."

It was Paul who helped Kathie to see that God had given her a unique talent, and that it was her mandate to be the best possible steward of that talent. She said, "We aren't to make excuses or deny the validity of a talent that is God-given; we must nourish and nurture that gift."

Kathie worked hard to establish a place for herself in the industry. The exuberant and talented singer landed the opportunity of singing on Ralph Edwards's "$100,000 Name That Tune." He testifies to the joy that characterizes Kathie's life:

"If Funk and Wagnall's or Webster's wants a sure three-word definition for the word *joy,* I offer this: *Kathie Lee Johnson.* Push it over, it bounces up joy. Sift it, strain it, grind it up; no matter what the pressure or temperature, turn on the blower, and it comes out joy.

"I've seen Kathie under the most trying conditions, cramming a rehearsal for a half-dozen or more songs on

'Name That Tune' into a brief period of concentration, honing all lyrics, remembering that the title of the song can only be 'la-la-la'd' so the contestant won't be told the tune. Then, after such a grueling, pounding period involving fifteen musicians, a leader, an arranger, an exacting show director, and a zoo of other necessities (make-up, wardrobe), I've seen her turn her cute little head—so fast her bouncy hair had to follow—spark up her polished dark brown eyes and with one word, or a look or embrace, or some prankish pantomine, turn what could be a high-tension moment into a tonic, a deceptive sneak attack on our hearts and funny bones, a gesture that says: 'Hey, I love you all.'

"Kathie seems to have understood, more than most people, what was meant in Psalms 100: 'Make a joyful noise unto the Lord, all ye lands. Serve the Lord with gladness: come before his presence with singing' (KJV).

"She has been doing that as long as my wife Barbara and I have known her and her wonderful Paul. I like to feel that Kathie Lee's joy is our Lord's honor medal, for I am sure it comes straight from him."

Kathie's zest for living is almost too much for some people to handle, and some have had trouble believing her enthusiasm was real. "I would get letters from viewers who would ask, 'Why do you love those contestants on the show? You're so bubbly. Are you on drugs?' " Kathie said.

The exuberance Kathie shows is real, but she does admit that "I've always been too proud to wear my heart on my sleeve in public. There is a part of me that has always said, 'I don't ever want to be a burden to people. I just want to be a blessing to everyone. The Lord had to reveal to me that it wasn't so much that I wanted to be a blessing, but that I didn't want anybody to think I had problems.

When I realized that, I started opening up to people I really trusted. If I'm feeling low, I spend time with the Lord, quietly, crying out to him and saying, 'Why me, Lord?' I get it all out so there aren't any walls around me, so he can then speak to me. He talks to me when I am in the bathtub, or when I am vacuuming. That's about the only time I'm not talking."

Kathie likens joy and the eight other fruit of the Spirit to marriage. "Unless you work at it everyday, it's not going to be there."

Sharing her faith in Jesus Christ comes as naturally to Kathie as the sun rising in the east. "None of us is alike, and that's what makes God's kingdom so interesting, but I think Christians who aren't joyful are a bad witness to the world. Someone with a long face who says, in a monotone, 'I want to tell you what Jesus means to me,' wouldn't interest most non-Christians. But sometimes my overabundance of joy or enthusiasm might seem to be too much. Everything in our Christian life needs to be balanced. Jesus wept. He didn't go around bubbling all the time. He got mad. It's his life we are to exemplify."

Kathie is a staunch believer in being the same on stage as off. "I want there to be a consistency in my life. The Lord has told me one percent of my ministry is on the stage; the rest is what I do and say offstage. When I was entertaining at Disney World, I made it a point to know all the waiters and waitresses by first name. I didn't just run off the stage and go to my dressing room and try to be alone. I knew getting to know them would make a much greater impact on their lives. Then when they see me giving my testimony on the '700 Club' or the 'Dinah Shore Show,' I pray that they'll know what I have said is for real."

Among her credits, the whirlwind of a singer has appeared in Las Vegas, was a regular on the "Hee Haw Honeys" TV show, and has put together a dinner theatre act, as well as displaying her vocal artistry on three record albums. In between, she squeezes in occasional concerts.

If her enthusiasm is waning before a show, she offers a simple prayer, "Lord Jesus, I'm not here for me anyway. I know that, so help me to see those people out there as you see them, give me your love for them, because my love right now is about a thimbleful. My joy is dried up, and I have no desire to go out on that stage. But I'm going to, because you require that of me. Then, the moment I step out there, my joy is real."

Through her example of expressing her joy in Jesus Christ before a vast audience or, on a personal level, while discipling a new Christian friend, Kathie epitomizes something she firmly believes in: "If we do what God requires of us, the joy comes immediately."

Carrie ten Boom

PEACE

Corrie ten Boom

In the film, *Apocalypse Now,* the villain, Kurtz, who is
driven insane by the evil he has embraced, explains, "There
are two choices with horror—you either make it your friend
or it overcomes you with fear." Was he right? Is there
not a third choice?

All of us face the darkness. Newspapers are filled with
stories of hate, rape, cynicism, murder, and war. And these
are supposedly days of peace and prosperity! The sickness
we see without is only evidence of the darkness within
the souls of men. Had Christ not come, then perhaps the
fictional Kurtz would be speaking the truth. But Christ
did come and "In Him was life; and the life was the light
of men. And the light shines in the darkness; and the darkness did not comprehend it" (John 1:4–5).

Before the resurrected Christ ascended to the Father,
he bequeathed a legacy of peace to all believers: "Peace
I leave with you; My peace I give to you; not as the world
gives, do I give to you. Let not your heart be troubled,
nor let it be fearful" (John 14:27).

Doesn't this capsulize the reasons a Christian is free from
the fear of evil and the damnation of guilt? Why he knows

joy, hope, and peace? Good overcame evil; Jesus is victor!

Peace is not just the absence of emotion. It is not just a hallowed feeling that sweeps over us at certain times. Henry Drummond says in his book, *The Greatest Thing in the World,* that "it [peace] is the perfect poise of the soul; the absolute adjustment of the inward man to the stress of all outward things; the preparedness against every emergency; the stability of assured convictions; the eternal calm of an invulnerable faith; the repose of a heart set deep in God. It is the mood of the man who says, with Browning, 'God's in His Heaven—all's well with the world.' "

Billy Graham wrote in his book, *Peace with God,* "The storm was raging. The sea was beating against the rocks in huge, dashing waves. The lightning was flashing, the thunder was roaring, the wind was blowing; but the little bird was asleep in the crevice of the rock, its head tucked serenely under its wing. That is peace—to be able to sleep in the storm!

"In Christ, we are relaxed and at peace in the midst of the confusions, bewilderments, and perplexities of this life. The storm rages, but our hearts are at rest. We have found peace—at last!"

In a world frantic for distractions from the real issues of life, and amid a population haunted by unnamed fears, the Christian can rest peacefully. For the true Christian is the one who has faced the issues . . . the threat of darkness without and the condemnation of darkness within . . . and has found the cure for it all—Christ.

Peace within ourselves comes to us only as we learn to trust God more and more. Craving for inner peace and security is universal, and the answer lies in "casting all your care upon him; for he careth for you" (1 Pet. 5:7, KJV).

Freed by confession and saved by faith, the believer is filled with light—the Holy Spirit. Peace blossoms from him and becomes precious, life-giving fruit in a starving world.

Horatio Gates Spafford knew the meaning of God's peace. His home was destroyed in the Great Chicago Fire. His beautiful possessions were gone, but not his family. Then later his wife and four daughters sailed for a visit to France. Their ship was rammed by an English vessel and two hundred twenty-six people, including his four daughters, drowned.

Spafford left for Europe to join his grief-stricken wife. His voyage was a lonely and heartbreaking one. The captain took him up on the deck one night to show him the spot where the ship had gone down.

Returning to his cabin, Spafford spent a night in prayer, pouring out his grief to the Lord. As he felt the comfort of Christ's love, Spafford wrote out of the despair of his dark experience:

> When peace, like a river, attendeth my way,
> When sorrows like sea-billows roll;
> Whatever my lot, thou hast taught me to say,
> "It is well, it is well with my soul."

Corrie ten Boom is another person who learned those simple promises of peace at an early age. Born into the ten Boom family in 1892, little Corrie became part of God's family by the turn of the century.

Life in the tiny watchshop in the heart of Haarlem, Holland—with its crammed living quarters above—was peace-filled. Days melted into years, and though Corrie's understanding of Scripture grew by leaps and bounds, her childlike faith never changed.

When Mama ten Boom died, the two spinster daughters, Betsie and Corrie, took her place in sharing the comfort of their home with all who came to their door. Though Corrie had become busy as a licensed watchmaker under her father's tutoring, she took time to reach out and offer her Savior's peace to the world around her. She ministered extensively to the mentally retarded children of the city. "Often," Corrie has said, "it was easier for these simple ones to grasp the truth of the gospel than for the highly intellectual person."

Corrie, who never married, knew to look to the Lord for fulfillment. Too often singles find themselves in a "holding pattern," discontented because they are not married. Through the tears and heartbreak of a romance early in her years, Corrie learned that a life of serenity and security in Christ is contingent upon putting him and his will first. Corrie, who deeply loves children, never had the pleasure of becoming a natural mother—but she cannot number the many God gave her the opportunity to lead into spiritual rebirth.

In addition to working with mentally retarded children, Corrie organized many clubs for girls. Not only did she provide recreation and training for the hundreds of girls who participated in these clubs; she also led many of them to Christ. When war arrived to shatter the tranquility of Dutch life, Corrie was glad she had given so many of "her girls" the knowledge of Christ. Many of them died in those years, and Jesus was for them a citadel of strength.

Could this same peace that sufficed for Corrie prior to 1939 be sufficient when the horror of the most evil war the world has ever known wrapped itself around Holland? Could she reach out with Christ's peace to the Nazi soldiers who marched down the tiny streets and into the little shops?

Proverbs 16:7 says, "When a man's ways are pleasing

to the Lord, He makes even his enemies to be at peace with him" (NAS). But to Corrie, at that time, the evil she was seeing around her justified the hatred she felt. It was only after many months, and many bitter experiences, that Corrie was willing to let the Lord cleanse her of that hatred.

After all, isn't hatred justified when you see millions of Jews—revered and loved by the ten Booms as God's chosen people—carted off to concentration camps, only to be exterminated? Corrie's love and prayers continued to bypass the Germans, extending to the Jews: "Lord Jesus, I offer myself for your people. In any way. Any place. Any time." Secular history books now record the results of Corrie's prayer that day as she stood in the cobbled marketplace. Her arms of love were soon embracing a large underground network committed to saving all the Jews it could. What some of the history books fail to tell is that, in addition to the hope and freedom she offered the Jews from their German enemies, she also offered a hope and freedom that could last through eternity.

Betrayal by a fellow Dutchman resulted in the arrest of Corrie and several members of her family. Most were released, but their father died, and Corrie and Betsie were sent to Ravensbruck concentration camp. The Apostle Paul, who knew of jails and hunger said, "I have learned to be content, whatever the circumstances may be" (Phil. 4:11, PHILLIPS). But could his experiences possibly compare to the filth, the stench, the hatred, and the mass killings of a concentration camp?

In prison Corrie's hatred seethed. Her peace was gone. But Betsie would open her tiny Bible for all who would listen, and her sister Corrie listened too. The reality of God's promises eventually stilled her heart. "No hate, Corrie," Betsie would say, and gradually love replaced hatred. Corrie's peace returned.

The peace that emanates from Corrie ten Boom, the peace that now has inspired millions around the globe, was forged into her soul under the shadow of the incinerators.

Corrie tells of the peace she felt even in the freezing predawn hours before prison roll call, when she and Betsie would walk over the frozen ground in the presence of the Lord. "Betsie would speak, then I would, and then the Lord. He would say a word, I don't know how. But we both understood him. And so it went, the three of us walking and talking there . . . a little bit of heaven in the midst of hell."

The Apostle Paul's words to the Ephesians burst with new life, "For he is our peace" (2:14, KJV). Corrie admits looking back on those hard days, "It was not my faith; oh no, my faith was weak, faltering. It was the Lord. He was there. I had only to rest in him."

Crammed in her tiny sleeping space, covered only partially by a thin blanket, Corrie remembered her father's tender hand on her face when he would tuck his little girl in bed. "Heavenly Father," she prayed, "let me feel thy hand upon my face now, until I sleep."

When fighting would break out in the barracks, providing the sadistic guards an opportunity to administer harsh discipline, Betsie and Corrie would pray. When they did, peace flowed in gentle waves across those hundreds of torn lives.

When the women were escorted to the shower chambers once a month, Corrie faced the nozzles calmly. She knew that the possibility of poisonous gas coming out was just as likely as that of receiving refreshing water.

"Thou wilt keep him in perfect peace, whose mind is stayed on thee: because he trusteth in thee" (Isa. 26:3,

KJV). Corrie had learned to trust. She knew her life was safe with Christ in God. Stripped of all other hope, she found that was enough.

When Betsie died, and Corrie was smuggled into the corpse-filled hospital room, she saw that her sister had glimpsed the joy just ahead of her. It was captured on Betsie's still face. It was then that Corrie fully realized how untouchable God's peace is. Not even death could mar it.

Weeks later, Corrie was released from prison and walked back into life, free. She was free from the unimportant frivolities, distractions, and concerns that usually hamper a Christian's witness. She had gone into the palaces of evil, and found Jesus is Lord—even there.

To live in peace implies that we have peace within ourselves. That personal peace can only come from our Creator, since it is not a natural characteristic. "Don't worry about anything; instead, pray about everything; tell God your needs and don't forget to thank him for his answers. . . . His peace will keep your thoughts and your hearts quiet and at rest as you trust in Christ Jesus" (Phil. 4:6–7, TLB).

I was present the first time Corrie saw the World Wide Pictures movie on her life, *The Hiding Place.* She found herself reliving the suffering of her family. She saw the cruelties of the concentration camp, and vividly remembered her father's and Betsie's deaths. As she left the tiny projection room at the studios, she began to cry softly. Few others noticed, but Ethel Waters was there, and sensitive to all Corrie was feeling. She gently put her arm around Corrie, and with her other hand soothingly wiped her brow. She quietly whispered, "Just cry, baby. Don't worry about the other people." I watched as Ethel ever so softly began to sing, just to Corrie, the song she had sung to audiences of thousands: "His eye is on the sparrow/And I know He watches me."

God used Ethel Waters that day to shower upon Corrie a special measure of peace when it was so much needed.

Corrie was fifty-three years old when she began her public ministry. Before she died, Betsie had been given a dream of their going all over the world to tell "of God's marvelous light. We will tell them there is not a pit so deep that God's love is not deeper still. They will believe us, because we have been here."

Thus commissioned, Corrie went. For nearly thirty-four years she "tramped the world" for Jesus Christ, living out of a suitcase. This grey-haired Dutch lady has entered the prisons of Africa, trekked through the mud of wartime Vietnam, carried Bibles behind the Iron Curtain, and entered the palaces of royalty—all with the name of Jesus on her lips and a sparkle in her blue eyes.

Each time Corrie spoke, peace flowed from her—the peace of God moving through the life of a child yielded and trusting in him. Up until the time heart problems slowed Corrie down, she never owned a home. How fitting that when "tramping" was no longer her Lord's command, the home he provided for her was christened "Shalom"—peace!

From her new home, Corrie continued conveying Christ's message of peace to the world. Through a number of books and the making of five films, her desire to let millions know of the Savior's love was fulfilled.

Even when she was silenced by a series of strokes, Corrie knew to rest in Jesus. Her "ministry without words" continued to reach out to others during difficult days of her illness. Nurses sent to help were helped in return—by a smile, the glow of her blue eyes, or the peaceful look on her face. Even during those days, the Spirit whose fruit had blossomed and matured in Corrie continued to plant life in others.

Pam Rosewell, Corrie's constant companion and secretary, witnessed the peace surrounding this woman of God. She says, "I had always seen the Lord Jesus Christ in Tante Corrie, but now I can see him even more clearly, and his life in her is a great reality. The days of her serious illness stretched into weeks, months, and now years, and she is entirely dependent upon others for every physical need. The peace of the Lord Jesus Christ is consistent and deep. Tante Corrie accepts her limitations, and although they are difficult can even laugh at some of the problems which can arise through lack of speech and mobility. This has a great effect on those who have the privilege of looking after her, and those who visit her. There is something more than noble about it; it is royal. It is the presence of the Prince of Peace himself."

Edgar Elfstrom, a close friend of Corrie's, told me about a special blessing God gave to her. Even though she could not form sentences—or even speak individual words—she could still sing word for word the hymns she learned as a child. And God enabled her to sing them not only in Dutch, but also in her learned language—English.

Corrie's life proves that the fictional Kurtz spoke a lie. There are not just two choices with horror. God never intended his children to enter hell. Jesus gave a third choice when he took the darkness to himself on the cross and bore the anguish of God's judgment. Only Jesus Christ had the infinite capacity to suffer so. But because he did, we don't ever walk through any valley of shadows alone. God has hid his children in Christ, and we are carried through in peace.

Joni Eareckson

PATIENCE

*The fruit of the Spirit is love,
joy, peace, PATIENCE. . . .*

Joni Eareckson

The frantic pace of our daily duties has turned the word *instant* into a cherished word—instant potatoes, instant credit, and instant success. We refuse to wait for anything these days unless there just is no other choice.

Anticipation is a lost art. We have been led to believe that anything we want we can have right now! The important lesson of working hard toward a goal and waiting diligently for the fruits of our labor has been lost to the "I-want-it-right-now" generation. The waiting process often hurts. It brings with it tensions, and if it goes on too long it leads to discouragement.

The Psalmist wrote: "Wait for the Lord; Be strong, and let your heart take courage; Yes, wait for the Lord" (Ps. 27:14).

But it's not always easy! You wait in line at the grocery store behind a woman whose cart makes it look like she is shopping for an entire army. Your blood pressure starts rising, and you find yourself getting angry both at her and at the slow cashier. Don't they know how valuable your time is?

All of us know what it means to experience that kind

of frustration, even though we know we should endure that frustration with patience. How often we have cried out to the Lord for patience because we have responded with angry words to some minor irritation.

God doesn't promise to remove the barriers of frustration from our lives, but he does promise to show us how we can bear up patiently against any trial. Romans 5:3 says "We can rejoice, too, when we run into problems and trials for we know that they are good for us—they help us learn to be patient. And patience develops strength of character in us and helps us trust God more each time we use it until finally our hope and faith are strong and steady" (TLB).

People can be exasperating, and sometimes it's hard to be patient with others. Yet Jesus is our example of proper patience. The impulsive Peter could have tried Jesus' patience, but instead the Master just loved him. Others of the disciples were also tough characters, and they let Jesus down more than once, but he went on loving them regardless.

That's the way it is today. It's too easy to neglect Christ, to rush ahead of him and to let him down, but in his unlimited patience he forgives and forgets.

The life of a Christian in the hands of God is like an arrow in the hands of a skilled archer. He points us toward something we cannot see, and the pressure mounts as he stretches and strains us to a point where we say, "I can't stand any more." He goes on stretching until his purpose for us is accomplished.

When we suffer we merely endure, but if we suffer with patience we endure calmly. That's the way Christ wants it to be.

Sometimes God allows us to suffer so that we will learn obedience. David learned obedience the hard way. Regarding his suffering he said, ". . . [it] was the best thing that could have happened to me, for it taught me to pay attention to your laws" (Ps. 119:71, TLB).

Patience perfects our Christian characters, and molds us into more Christlike people. James 1:2–4 says "Is your life full of difficulties and temptations? Then be happy, for when the way is rough, your patience has a chance to grow. So let it grow, and don't try to squirm out of your problems. For when your patience is finally in full bloom, then you will be ready for anything, strong in character, full and complete" (TLB).

Though Joni Eareckson is only thirty-one years old, she will never walk again, nor will she ever use her hands to brush her teeth or comb her hair. Yet, more than any other friend I know, she exemplifies patience in "full bloom" as described in James.

She must wait until someone can come to get her out of bed in the mornings and then bathe and dress her. Whatever her needs are—twenty-four hours a day—Joni must rely on others.

Patience didn't develop overnight for Joni. It took but a fleeting second for her exciting teenage world to crumble into what seemed like a hopeless and worthless existence, but it has taken much longer for her to come to terms with her vastly altered life.

On a hot, humid July afternoon in 1967, Joni and her sister Kathy hurried to Chesapeake Bay for a quick swim before the sun went down. Two months before, Joni had been voted "most athletic" by her graduating class at Woodlawn High School in Maryland. The seventeen-year-old girl had excelled at field hockey and had won blue ribbons riding her horse Tumbleweed. Diving and swimming came naturally to her. That day a perfect jackknife from a raft into the murkey shallow waters sent her crashing into the bottom, severing her spinal cord. Kathy dragged the limp body to shore, and within minutes a screeching ambulance rushed the injured Joni to University Hospital.

The doctors diagnosed a broken neck. It took time for the severity of the accident to register with Joni, but when it did she was filled with a tremendous fear of dying. Later the thought of never being able to walk again—of being a quadriplegic—was even more frightening than that of dying.

The days blurred into months as she lay motionless in a Stryker Frame—a two-sided canvas frame which allowed her to be flipped every two hours.

If there had been a way for her to kill herself, she would have—but without the use of her hands she couldn't take pills. She begged her best friend to slash her wrists, saying there would be no pain. Her friend refused. Anger, depression, and frustration almost overwhelmed her.

Joni had trusted her life to Christ at a Young Life Camp, but now her circumstances raised a lot of questions about God. Was he to blame for this accident? Was this his way of punishing her for past sins? How could anything good come from her accident? As she lay still between the two white sheets, she often cried out in despair, "God, how could you be so cruel as to make me spend the rest of my life like this?"

Family and friends spent many hours at the hospital trying to cheer her. At first she would scoff when they would quote Scripture verses like "The Lord says He will never allow us to suffer more than we can bear."

As she began to let go of her own emotions, to trust God and his ways, she finally began to see that even so-called bad things fit together into a pattern for good. She found hope in the verse "And we know that God causes all things to work together for good to those who love God, to those who are called according to His purpose" (Rom. 8:28, NAS).

Joni now says, "Our problem is that we just think of good as it affects us in the here and now. We think of good in terms of smiles and happiness and giddiness and fun and games, wealth and material blessings, ease, comfort, and prosperity. But God has a different kind of good in store for us. His idea of good is how it will affect us in eternity."

Joni's boyfriend Dick gave her a Bible with large print that, when it was placed on the floor beneath her Stryker Frame, she could read and study until she needed a page turned.

She began to comprehend from Scripture that God had allowed her accident to happen for a purpose. He wanted to test her faith and spiritual endurance. Through her he wanted to reach out with his love to others who were also suffering.

For Joni, God did not choose to do a physical healing. In its place the Holy Spirit taught her patience and granted her a spiritual healing which has allowed her to touch countless lives for him.

Joni loved to study in the Bible about the prophets and apostles who had suffered, because she could learn so much from them. Hadn't Jeremiah had his share of trials? Didn't Paul endure beatings as well as ill health? Wasn't Jesus paralyzed as he suffered on the cross between two thieves?

But most of all Joni related to Job. He too was full of questions when he asked God, "Why are you allowing this pain and these problems to happen to me?" Joni says, "As I studied the book of Job, I discovered that not once did God come to Job's side and sit down next to him and say, 'I'm going to explain to you the ins and outs of why I am letting you go through all of this.' No, God never did that. In fact, God had a few questions for Job. He said, 'Job, where were you when I laid the foundations of this earth? Do you understand the majesty of the horse or the might of the ox? Do you know where the sun comes from? Do you understand how I've set stars and moons spinning in motion? Do you know how I puckered up mountain ranges or ladled out the seas? Do you understand or can you tell me how I dreamed up time and space and your very existence?' Job probably scratched his head in bewilderment and thought to himself, 'Well now, Lord, I don't know the answer to those things. I don't know anything about nature. I only want a few answers to my questions about pain.' But it was almost as though God was saying to Job, 'Look, you can't even understand the ins and outs of nature. How are you going to understand the way in which I deal with you in a spiritual dimension?' "

As Joni continued to study, she began to see that wisdom did not necessarily mean figuring out the blueprint for her future. Wisdom was trusting God and waiting on him.

Longsuffering—patience—is a quality that does not surrender to circumstances. Joni learned that God could use her despite the fact that she could not walk or use her hands, that he wanted to make her more Christlike. She believes that's his will for every one of us Christians. "Thank the Lord we don't all have to break our necks to find that out. God will allow pain to touch our hearts so that we might learn to depend on him. What better time to depend on him than when you have to? Then you really get to know him. The fruit of the Spirit becomes evident in your life. You see a difference. You see, feel, touch, and taste his sustaining grace in such a way that you never imagined when you languished around in your bed of roses."

Joni worked hard in rehabilitation. Therapists had to manipulate her limbs so that they would not shrivel up. What were once natural responses—even sitting up—had to be learned all over again.

In therapy Joni was shown how to use her shoulder muscles and thereby to move her arms. She learned an early lesson in patience when she was placed in an electric wheelchair and was challenged by her physical therapist to "meet me in occupational therapy."

"But that's not scheduled for two hours," Joni reminded her as she surveyed the short distance of thirty feet. But every minute became a battle as Joni struggled to use those muscles to manipulate the lever. With much determination, she arrived exhausted at her destination barely within the two hours. "Only champs go the distance," the therapist encouraged her.

Joni constantly hoped the Lord was going to heal her, and she often prayed for it to happen right away. "I don't see life as God does," Joni told her friend Diana. "That's why I get impatient. A year here seems like forever, but that isn't much time to God."

About the time Joni was ready to give up, having learned that she would never use her hands again, a therapist suggested she try to learn to write and draw with a pen in her mouth. She had had artistic talent before the accident, and even though drawing with a pen in her mouth sounded disgusting, it was worth a try.

The lines were squiggly at first. The work was tedious. If she dropped the pen she had to wait for someone to pick it up and place it back in her mouth. It took months of patience and determined practice just to control the movement of the pen.

Often her jaw would get tired, and she could only work a few minutes at a time because the close work was a strain on her eyes. One slip of the pen after many hours would ruin an entire drawing. But gradually she learned that ability was in her brain, not in her hands. Attractive pictures of horses and other scenes she remembered from her family's Maryland farm began to take form.

By not giving up, Joni began to produce art of a professional quality, and soon she was turning her work into a successful business venture. One of her drawings won first prize at an art show—and the judges never knew it was drawn by a quadriplegic.

Finally, after more than two years of being in hospitals and rehabilitation centers, Joni was able to go home. She continued to study God's Word, and began to accept herself and her life in a wheelchair. She realized it was OK not to like being paralyzed, and that it was OK to cry, because paralysis was not God's ultimate plan for her.

"God promises me a new, glorified body—hands that will work and feet that will walk. I'm not going to always be in this wheelchair. But for now God has given me the power not only to live and to cope successfully in it, but to smile about it and actually find some good things," Joni says.

As Joni's drawings became more popular, news of the quadriplegic artist traveled to the producers of the "Today Show," and she was invited to be a guest. Executives at Zondervan Publishing House saw the young girl interviewed by Barbara Walters, and contacted her about writing a book—another task that took a lot of patience.

Joni, who thought only her friends would read the book, was surprised when the honesty of her story touched millions. Her schedule was soon filled with speaking engagements, as she shared the lessons she learned about patience and suffering. "We all have a handicap—maybe not a broken neck, but maybe a broken heart, loneliness, sorrow, or grief. God tells us not to try to escape our problems and pain, but come to him first and let him deal with it."

World Wide Pictures saw that, through the medium of film, Joni could be an inspiration to many. Here was the story of a young woman who had conquered depression when it would have been so easy to give up, a story of painful struggle and eventual victory to share with millions.

Joni was thrilled her story would be made into a movie, but she wasn't quite so sure about it when Bill Brown, the president of World Wide Pictures, called her at her Sykesville home with the idea that she play herself in the film. With a yell that could almost be heard without the phone across the continent she screamed, "Have you gone bananas? I'm not an actress, and for another thing I just don't know whether I could go through it again."

Joni was coaxed to come to Los Angeles for a screen test before the final decision was to be made. When the director Jim Collier saw the results of the screen test, there was no doubt in his mind that Joni should play herself. No actress could so fully understand the meaning of the words, "Lord, I wish I were on my feet again." For Joni that didn't take acting ability—it was her everyday feeling.

Back home Joni prayed about her decision. She began to see that, if the real person were on the screen saying the real lines, the message of the film would have a greater impact.

By July, 1978, Joni was back in California to begin the fourteen-week shooting schedule. Even though she knew nothing of the movie industry, she quickly caught on. The crew and cast immediately fell in love with the vivacious leading lady.

One of the cameramen, Bob Marta, at first didn't want to work on a picture about a kid in a wheelchair; he thought it would be too depressing. However, once he met Joni, all his doubts fled, and in the months of working on the film he didn't consider Joni handicapped. In getting to know Joni and her family, Bob saw something he was missing. He realized his life needed turning around, and he accepted Christ.

It was one thing for Joni to write about her past for a book, but it was a much greater emotional strain to relive those frustrations and hurts for the cameras.

"I thought I wouldn't mind it at all," Joni says. "But when I got back on a Stryker Frame and they strapped the top on and turned me over, I really felt paralyzed. It hadn't felt that way since the early years when I struggled with my self-image. At times it was painfully real. I had thought those years were behind me, but there I was caught up in it again," she continues. "It was a cleansing experience. There were some old wounds that were never properly healed."

One particular incident in the filming that really tried Joni's patience was a scene when she was in intensive care in the hospital. Her boyfriend Dick sneaked past the nurses' station with a tiny puppy concealed in his jacket. The make-up man had Joni done up in pale white make-up to make her look very sick. She had on a wig that was partly shaven so that metal tongs would adhere to her head to stretch her neck and help it mend properly. Everything was portrayed accurately, and the director was ready for the cameras to roll. The actor, Cooper Huckabee, crawled on his knees past the nurses and into Joni's room. He got on the floor beneath the Stryker Frame where Joni lay face down. The script said, "dog licks Joni's face." Obviously the dog hadn't studied his lines. He refused to cooperate.

"Cut," the director yelled. The boyfriend and nurses got back to their original positions, and the scene was tried again. Take after take was tried but that cute puppy couldn't get his part right. He finally was replaced by another cuddly puppy. The stand-in dog also refused to play the role the way the director insisted.

Joni says, "Hour after hour of failure in filming, and I began to feel a little paranoid. I knew I looked ugly with the icky white make-up and the frightful wig. Evidently the dog got the message too, because he wouldn't lick my face."

The prop man smeared Gerber liver baby food on Joni's cheek, hoping to entice the puppy to lick. He obviously didn't like liver, because he still refused to cooperate. Finally, after sixteen takes, the puppy got his act together and licked Joni's face. The cast and crew were ecstatic because the scene was completed and they could go home.

But by this time Joni was beginning to feel weary. She said, "It was one of those times when I felt so ugly. I felt so paralyzed and rejected—by a dog of all things. I just wished I were out of there and safely back home."

The technicians scurried off, and Joni was put back into her wheelchair and taken to her second-floor dressing room. Then the tears flooded down her cheeks and over the crusty baby food. Soon she was sobbing uncontrollably. "God opened some old wounds," she says.

She was unable to divorce herself from the pain of that scene as she went home that night. As she went to bed, she began to go over some of the things she had learned in the past twelve years. "In Ecclesiastes it says there is a time to weep, a time to mourn, and I'm not supposed to feel ashamed if sometimes the limitations of this paralysis get to be too much. It's God's way of assuring me not to get too used to this wheelchair, because one day I'll be whole again."

Joni's story of how she fought a battle against depression, rage, and despair is now a major motion picture. As I returned to my home in Los Angeles after attending the world premiere of the film *Joni* in her hometown of Baltimore, the pilot flew the jet over Chesapeake Bay and announced the beautiful view to our right. "So that's where it all began," I thought to myself. "That murky water and shallow bottom was where my friend Joni's life changed from that of an active teenager to that of a quadriplegic destined to years in a wheelchair. God refined the life of that young woman and allowed her to touch countless others through her artwork, books, speaking engagements, and now her film.

Joni taught me that God allows pain and problems to push our eyes away from the passing things of this earth and draw them upward. We may not be able to control our circumstances, but the way we respond to them will determine the richness of our inheritance in eternity.

We cannot hurry God but we can wait—with patience—and that's all he asks.

Norma Zimmer

KINDNESS

The fruit of the Spirit is love, joy,
peace, patience, KINDNESS. . . .

Norma Zimmer

Kindness is love in action, and don't be surprised if you find it is contagious.

As I watched the cars whizzing by me one day on the busy California freeway, I helplessly looked at my car with its flat tire. A gentleman stopped and offered his assistance. Appreciative but a little hesitant to infringe on his time, I said I hated to see him troubled with the effort to change my tire. His comment: "I had car trouble once, and a kind man stopped by to help me. I want to be able to pass that along."

Stephen De Grellet once said, "I expect to pass through this world but once; any good thing therefore that I can do, or any kindness that I can show to any fellow-creature, let me do it now; let me not defer or neglect it, for I shall not pass this way again."

Christ's life was spent in doing kind deeds and making people happy. Someone once said, "The greatest thing a man can do for his heavenly Father is to be kind to his other children."

Kindness can be expressed in simple ways—a smile, a handshake, a greeting card, or a thank-you note. The telephone company's commercial says, "reach out and touch someone," and, whether it's a call or a card, your effort says you care. The way we treat others expresses our inward qualities.

When we as Christians let the Holy Spirit grow the fruit of kindness in our lives, we must be willing to endure a little inconvenience, to go the extra mile and to be willing to do so often without recognition.

The Apostle Paul expresses in Ephesians 4:32 the law of personal relationships: "Be kind to one another." Kindness is a deed expressed without expecting a reward in return. Often the act will go unnoticed, or so we think, and we wonder if it was really worth our efforts. But kindness and helpfulness reduce stress in our own lives, as well as making others' lives a little more bearable.

Queen Victoria visited the injured soldiers who were brought back from the ravages of war. She was distressed by one wounded man. "Is there anything I can do for you?" she questioned the young man. "Nothing, your majesty, unless you would thank my nurse for her kindness to me," he replied.

Colossians 3:12 exhorts the believers to "put on a heart of compassion, kindness, humility, gentleness and patience." This tells us that kindness is not a quality of human nature but a fruit that we must cultivate to its fullest. Kindness needs to be taught to young children.

There are times, however, when what seems an act of kindness is not really kind. To overlook a fault is not always being kind, and neither is it kindness to overlook a child's wrong deed. The Holy Spirit can give discernment as to when kindness should be tender or tough.

The Lord's example of kindness is the goal for which we should strive. Psalms 34:8 says, "Oh, put God to the test and see how kind he is! See for yourself the way his mercies shower down on all who trust in him" (TLB).

An example of Jesus' kindness is displayed in John 4 when he, weary from his journey, stopped to rest by Jacob's well. He asked a Samaritan woman for a drink. The woman was surprised that a Jew would speak to a "despised Samaritan"; besides, this woman had a terrible reputation. But nevertheless Jesus spoke to her.

It was important that he spoke, but what he had to say was even more significant. He did not condemn her. He did not belittle her for her failures. He asked her for a drink and spoke words of hope. He kindly allowed her to maintain some dignity and to feel a sense of worth.

King David praised the Lord in Psalms 117 and said, "His lovingkindness is great toward us" (NAS), and in Psalms 23:6 he realized that "goodness and lovingkindness will follow me all the days of my life." First Corinthians 13 expresses that "love is kind."

Kindness should have been Norma Zimmer's middle name. She showers it upon everyone.

The first time I met Norma was at a Billy Graham Crusade in Portland, Oregon. She stopped by the office where I was working, and that contagious smile I had seen so often on the "Lawrence Welk Show" greeted me. Her "hello" was so warm that I felt like I had known her for years.

That was the first of scores of crusades at which she would sing, and our paths began to cross occasionally. Void of the standard Hollywood "celebrity mentality," Norma never expected the VIP treatment. I've seen her ride to the airport in the back seat of a van with luggage piled around her.

Early in our friendship, I remember an act of kindness from Norma. She sent me a Christmas card with a handwritten note saying, "Would you ever have time to have lunch with me?" Would *I* have time to have lunch with this busy recording artist, wife, mother, and grandmother? The gracious lady knew that kindness does not take anyone for granted.

Marcy Tigner, a good friend of Norma's, clued me in to Norma's secret for always being ready to do a kind deed. Marcy said, "Norma's close walk with the Lord keeps her filled with his love. Is it any wonder that she shows so much love and kindness to others? She is the same whether things are going well or whether there are problems and disappointments. As I became better acquainted with her, I found that there is a reason for her loving disposition. She depends upon the Lord in every situation. I have seen her constantly turn to God's Word to find the answers to various problems. Norma loves to read the Bible."

Perhaps Norma learned the importance of kindness as a youngster, when it was often shown to her. She tells of kind landlords that never pushed her family for rent during difficult financial days, of teachers who cared about her, of neighbors who helped her.

Norma was the youngest of three children born to the Larsens in Idaho. Her father, a talented violinist, found it difficult to hold on to a job. The family moved to Tacoma, Washington, and from then on into a series of tenement houses and shanties. Mr. Larsen turned to drinking for comfort, and by the time Norma was ten her mother was also an alcoholic.

School was difficult for Norma; the other kids made fun of her hand-me-down clothes, and when her parents were drunk they caused embarrassment for the shy girl. But her second-grade teacher singled her out for many acts of kindness which were very important to the youngster. "I sensed she cared, and probably knew what our home life was like," Norma said of the memory that is now etched in her mind.

Norma vividly remembers a Thanksgiving when the neighbors wanted to express kindness to the Larsen family but their generosity was refused. "It was 1932 and a hard winter," Norma says. "We were suffering from malnutrition, and I think I was close to starvation. I was too weak to stand. The day before the holiday, several ladies knocked on our door, and Dad answered. 'We brought you a turkey,' a lady cheerfully greeted Dad. He refused their hospitality, throwing the turkey on the ground and screaming, 'I don't want charity.' We had bread that Thanksgiving."

Mr. Larsen endeavored to teach all of his children the music he loved so much. Norma was eager to please him, and learned much from the talented musician. Along with her brother and sister, Norma joined the choir of the University Christian Church near their home in Seattle, Washington. It was there that she first heard and believed in Jesus Christ. And she began to let Christ be the Lord of her life, she began to see herself developing a new, healthier self-image.

The music director at the church was also a teacher at her school. He offered her a scholarship to study voice with him privately. "There is no way I can ever repay him for his many kindnesses to me," Norma says, "so I give thanks to God and use my training for him." The soloist, in repaying her music director's kindness, has given the world her beautiful songs, and through them has shared Christ's love wherever she goes.

A girlfriend gave Norma a birthday gift of an overnight cruise to Victoria, British Columbia, in Canada. On the trip home, a passenger started singing, and before long the others joined in. A man seated next to Norma heard her clear voice and asked her to sing a solo. For over two hours Norma sang every song she knew to the delight of the entire ship. One of the passengers was a Hollywood agent, and offered her an audition if she ever were in

Los Angeles. His kindness started her on her musical career.

Soon she was able to make that trip and to establish contacts that were vital in the entertainment industry. She joined a trio called the Tailor Maids and, believing no job was too small, substituted for various groups. This gave her exposure in the profession.

Meanwhile, Randy Zimmer, a handsome, rugged athlete Norma had met on the ski slopes in the state of Washington, missed the petite young lady and followed her to Los Angeles. In June, 1944, the couple was married in a tiny wedding chapel with borrowed flowers and candles.

Norma's career as a singer blossomed, and for over seventeen years she worked doing background music with well-known musicians. She sang theme songs for motion pictures, did weekly radio programs, and warbled hundreds of jingles for commercials. After Norma had done backup work, including a short solo, for a Lawrence Welk album, she was asked to appear on his TV show. Norma was thrilled with the opportunity and the audience immediately took to her. The number of cards and letters was overwhelming, and Welk asked her back. On his New Year's Eve program in 1960, in front of TV cameras, he invited the stunned Norma to be a permanent member of his musical family.

When Ava Barber, the country-western singer on the show, moved to Los Angeles from her native Tennessee, she found a real friend in Norma. "When I would talk with Hollywood people, I found their minds would often drift away. Norma always took time to listen to me. If she had to leave to do her song, she would promise to come back, and she always did. She showed a real interest in any problem I had, and listened with concern. I just love her to death," Ava says in her Southern drawl.

Norma always takes time to care about her audiences.

Unless it is absolutely necessary, she never leaves one of her concerts without staying to sign autographs for everyone who asks.

An acquaintance of mine told me about getting Norma's autograph and the impression the singer made on her life. One year, as Norma was getting ready to ride a float in the world-famous Rose Bowl Parade, the autograph collector handed Norma an autograph book to sign. The collector was used to a quick scribble by the celebrity without any sign of recognition. Norma, however, took the time to look the lady in the eye and ask, "What songs do you like to hear on the Welk show?" The woman, a little surprised by her warm response, said, "I like it when you sing the gospel songs."

"That's my favorite too," Norma sweetly replied. The woman, who had collected hundreds of famous signatures, has never forgotten Norma's kindness and caring spirit.

To the entire Zimmer family, kindness comes as naturally as breathing. Norma and Randy and their son Mark took time to have dinner with me one evening, even though they were leaving at six o'clock the next morning to catch a plane for Birmingham, Alabama, where it is a Thanksgiving tradition for Norma to sing with the symphony.

Mark, the younger of the two Zimmer boys, told me his mother is constantly doing deeds of kindness. "She doesn't do them for a reward or to be noticed, so I really can't tell you a lot of examples. Often the recipient is the only one who knows," Mark told me.

Mark had often been the recipient, and remembered how his mother would always see that the kids had the best seat—whether at a concert where she would give up her own seat, or in a car, where she would climb in the back.

The bachelor Mark reflected back to his recent bout with hepatitis and said, "Mom would come over to my house every day to massage my feet and bring me something to eat. Even though she had lots to do, she was there, even when there was the danger of her catching the highly contagious disease."

With Randy's permission, Norma's mother came to live the Zimmers for many years. Norma, forgetting her unpleasant childhood memories, loved to buy her mother the fashionable clothing, jewelry, and other things she had missed when the Larsens lived in poverty. Selfishness has never been a part of Norma's life.

Randy's father also lived nearby. In his ailing years, Norma would go to his home in their mobile home park in La Habra and read the Bible to him each day.

Good motives alone do not guarantee good conduct. It's one thing to have good intentions, but another thing to put the feeling into action.

Without a moment's hesitation, Norma acts on her feelings of kindness and love. Everett and Marcy Tigner told me of one such incident. As the Tigners vacationed in Hawaii, their electricity went off, and consequently all the food in their refrigerator—including meat and fish—spoiled.

"The stench was awful," Marcy later said, and added it took weeks for the smell to completely disappear.

While the Tigners were still gone, one of their neighbors realized the problem and called Norma for advice. Without coming up with excuses, Norma arrived at the Tigner's home with her apron on, and worked for hours throwing out rotten food and scrubbing down the smelly refrigerator.

William Wordsworth could easily have been describing Norma Zimmer when he wrote:

> That best portion of a good man's life,
> His little, nameless, unremembered acts
> Of kindness and of love.

Mary C. Crowley

GOODNESS

The fruit of the Spirit is love, joy,
peace, patience, kindness,
GOODNESS. . . .

Mary C. Crowley

Goodness is closely related to kindness. *Chrēstotēs,* the Greek word used for kindness, refers to a kindly disposition, and *Agathōsunē,* the word Paul used for goodness, refers to a kindly activity. Kindness can only help, while goodness might—and can—discipline and correct.

Goodness is not necessarily done by gentle means; the person who would show goodness often is forced to use stern qualities. Jesus demonstrated goodness when he entered the temple, cast out all who were buying and selling, and overturned the tables of the money changers (Matt. 21:12–13).

We will be remembered for what we have done for others. The action-Christian will seek opportunities to be of service. Abraham Lincoln said at Gettysburg, "The world will little note, nor long remember, what *we say* here, but it can never forget what *they did* here" (italics mine).

Mother Teresa of Calcutta has turned her love into energy. Going into India from her native Yugoslavia, the faithful lady has spent her life caring for the sick and the dying, and fearlessly ministering to the victims of leprosy. Her work bridges caste and color, region and religion. The 1979 Nobel Peace Prize was awarded to Mother Teresa, and she accepted it in the name of the poor. This dedicated, frail woman serves the poor out of ultimate compassion. Her purpose is to show the world that each person, regardless of circumstances, has his own dignity that must be upheld.

Selfishness comes naturally, but goodness, like the other spiritual fruit, is grown by the Holy Spirit from within. Goodness springs forth in an honest and genuine way if we let it.

Goodness describes that which is good in its character but is also beneficial in its effect. Genuine goodness is not the good works done to gain recognition. Goodness overflows from a full heart; it involves passing on that with which Christ has blessed us to those needing an injection of God's lovingkindness.

The Living Bible so clearly tells the parable of Christ's goodness found in Matthew 20: "The owner of an estate went out early one morning to hire workers for his harvest field. He agreed to pay them $20 a day and sent them out to work.

"A couple of hours later he was passing a hiring hall and saw some men standing around waiting for jobs, so he sent them also into his fields, telling them he would pay them whatever was right at the end of the day."

At noon, three o'clock and at five o'clock he was still sending more unemployed men into his fields. That evening the paymaster paid all the men equally, but the ones who had been hired first protested when their pay was the same as that of those who had only worked a few hours.

" 'Friend,' he answered one of them, 'I did you no

wrong! Didn't you agree to work all day for $20? Take it and go. It is my desire to pay all the same; is it against the law to give away my money if I want to? Should you be angry because I am kind?' "

"Be ready for every good deed" (Titus 3:1). Being ready means being constantly alert for opportunities to do good, even if the occasion arises suddenly. The task may be minute, or it might be enormous, but a ready person doesn't procrastinate doing either.

Jesus also tells the parable of a man who called together his servants and loaned them money to invest for him while he went to another country. Verse 29 of Matthew 25 says, "For the man who uses well what he is given shall be given more, and he shall have abundance" (TLB).

Mary C. Crowley, founder and president of Home Interiors and Gifts, proved to God she was faithful in little things when she struggled during the Depression to support her two children.

Now, as head of a multimillion-dollar corporation, she says, "I am like the man who was once asked, 'How can you give away so much and have so much left?' He replied, 'I do not know—maybe it is like this: I shovel it out and God shovels it in. He has a bigger shovel than I have!' "

Mary, raised by Christian grandparents in Missouri, wasn't afraid of hard work, and her determination and optimism was second to none. Jobs were almost impossible to find during the Depression, but the young lady convinced a department store owner to give her a one-day trial as a sales clerk. Her enthusiasm was infectious as she set about devising a scheme for selling thread to the customers. She would say, "For only a penny more you can have a spool of thread, and you wouldn't have to wait for your change to come through the cash conveyor." This gimmick worked for Mary, and she not only was hired for a permanent job, but she soon was earning the dollar bonus for the biggest sales of the week.

With eagerness to better herself, Mary began to take classes in Dallas with the aid of a scholarship. To support her family, she also worked for an insurance company.

The aggressive lady had been taught the value of tithing, and on her meager income made a commitment to God to give 10 percent of her salary to her church, even though that meant no money in reserve for Christmas presents or miscellaneous bills. While her children looked on, Mary would fill her pledge envelope with her tithe and listen to them grumble about wishing for a new bicycle or yearning for a steak dinner rather than the breakfast cereal they just had for dinner.

"Sometimes it took a lot of praying," Mary says of stuffing that money in the offering envelope. But God saw to it that her needs were met, and there was plenty of love and mutual respect in her household.

While working for the insurance company, Mary met Dave Crowley, and after his stint with the armed forces overseas they were married.

Her continuing education led her to a job as an accountant, but in 1949 she met Mary Kay, the woman who later formed Mary Kay Cosmetics. Mary Kay encouraged her friend to try direct selling with the Stanley Corporation. The challenge was just what Mary needed, and within a few years she was using her selling expertise for another company, an importer. In three years, Mary had built the company into a successful business. However, differences in management techniques left Mary without a job.

The words Mary had once heard from a black preacher in Jamaica returned to haunt her: "God doesn't take time to make a nobody." With her husband's permission, Mary set out to form her own company for selling home accessories. The determined lady had to approach three different banks in order to get the needed six-thousand-dollar loan, but finally, in December, 1957, Home Interiors and Gifts, Inc. was started. Within five years, Home Interiors had over a million dollars in sales.

Today, Mary Crowley doesn't sit around waiting for goodness to be dropped into her lap; she believes in being the doer. "I can't outgive the Lord," she says. "If I only give to receive I am merely swapping, not giving." God has an abundance of good things, and Mary's philosophy is to think the best—"Think Mink."

The key to Mary's success is that she learned to trust God. "Too often we want to hold on to things ourselves— our anxiety and selfishness—but the Bible says we are to completely trust in the Lord," she says.

Mary sees each of the women who work for her as important people. This company's managers are taken to her mountain lodge in Colorado for a retreat where she teaches them from the book of Proverbs. Mary not only shares with the ladies how to be more effective saleswomen, but also how to be fulfilled persons.

The first year Home Interiors was in business, Mary decided to pay a small dividend on the stock and to give bonuses to the office staff and managers. In doing so, she was going against the advice of her accountant; "We won't have any reserve if you do," he warned her.

"It all depends on what you consider reserve," Mary replied. "I call it people and you call it money." Mary's goodness that year only bonded her employees together and made them determined to work harder for the company.

Home Interiors continued to grow as the enterprising woman ignited each employee's enthusiasm and set her goals high. The motto on her desk reads: "Attempt something so great that it is bound to fail unless God is in it."

Mary's compassionate spirit also reached into the handicapped community. Her son, Don, who is vice-president of her company, heard that the Caruth Rehabilitation Center was urging companies to hire the deaf. He hired one deaf person, who turned out to be a steady, reliable worker, so he hired another and another. News traveled quickly, and soon other handicapped people came seeking employment. By 1970 Home Interiors employed seventy-five crippled or deaf workers, including Vietnam veterans. Soon Mary helped the handicapped form their own company called Handi-Hands, which is a division of Home Interiors.

As Don's birthday approached one year, Mary pondered what to give her son. She wanted it to be something he would enjoy and that would at the same time benefit others. Don had learned firsthand the goodness spread by the Fellowship of Christian Athletes at their conference in Estes Park, Colorado. That sparked an idea in Mary to start a scholarship fund in his honor to send boys from all across America to the conferences. When the managers of Home Interiors heard of her gift to her son, they too wanted to be a part of it. Before long, the scholarship fund grew to over fifty thousand dollars.

Mary gets excited when she realizes that God has given her the unique experience of serving others by sharing what he has given her. "I learned long ago the thrill of sharing my earned money in a creative way—it doubles my enjoyment," she says.

As the holiday season approached in 1974, headlines screamed gloom and depression. Home Interiors had had a good year and the president again wanted to share the profits with those who had made it possible. Don came up with the idea of a shopping spree for all the employees in addition to the regular Christmas party with gifts and the bonuses. The idea was to take everyone to a local supermarket and to give them an hour to fill their carts. Home Interiors would foot the bill.

On the appointed day, employees boarded chartered buses to the Safeway store. There were smiles, tears, and flying hands as they hurried through the aisles, loading their carts. One of the newly married men was unaccustomed to grocery shopping, and Mary tipped him off that sugar was a good buy, as well as canned hams and salmon. The best shopper stuffed thirty-two sacks of groceries in his basket. The entire grocery bill came to forty-thousand-dollars.

Only a small news item about the event appeared in the Dallas newspapers, but phones began ringing at Home Interiors the next day. Television networks wanted to film the next shopping spree, scheduled for the employees at McKinney, Texas. That shopping spree found employees dodging cameramen and rolling their carts over electrical wires.

The good news and the positive outlook were telecast and reported all over the world as a refreshing antidote to the bad news filling the airwaves. "I never enjoyed spending $71,165 so much," said Mary. But the comment that thrilled her the most was that of an employee: "They're Christian people who don't just say it. They do it."

"The Holy Spirit nudges us to show goodness to others," Mary says. "We must always be sensitive to others' needs. If we can help others get what they want out of life, then we will get what we want."

Ethel Waters met Mary during the Billy Graham Crusade in Dallas, and the two felt an immediate kinship. Several years later, when Mary was in Los Angeles for a conference, she phoned Ethel, only to discover the singer was in poor physical health and not eating properly.

"I'm coming right over to visit you," Mary insisted, and she brought along a prime-rib dinner with all the trimmings. Ethel, who had known fame and acclaim, was deeply impressed by the generosity of this busy lady. After Ethel had eaten, she softly began to sing:

"I'm going to LIVE the way He wants me to live,
I'm going to GIVE until there's just no more to give,
I'm going to LOVE, love 'til there's just no more love,
I could never, never outlove the LORD."

Years later I accompanied Ethel to Dallas; Mary had invited her to sing that Gaither song at a special dedication service at First Baptist Church. Mary's generosity had made it possible for First Baptist to begin construction on a new structure, which they named the Mary C. Building.

I also witnessed firsthand the goodness of Mary when our mutual friend was confined to City of Hope Hospital. Painfully ill and near death, Ethel found it difficult to get used to the many different nurses that came into her room. Mary sent checks to cover the cost of having private nurses around the clock, thereby easing Ethel's troubled mind.

Colossians 1:10 says, "Always please the Lord and honor him, so that you will always be doing good, kind things for others, while all the time you are learning to know God better and better" (TLB).

"When God's children are in need, you be the one to help them out" (Rom. 12:13, TLB).

Mary listens to the promptings of the Holy Spirit to meet needs. Actor Tom Lester, a good friend of Mary's, once mentioned to her the needs of his small, struggling church, which was financially unable to support a pastor.

"We're a lighthouse in an area that so desperately needs the gospel," Tom told Mary. She immediately sent a check to help, and pledged to support that church monthly.

Anyone who knows Mary knows of her goodness. An evangelist in Texas was asked if he had ever heard of the gracious lady. "Oh, yes, I know her," he immediately replied, "she's the one who keeps my ministry going."

Peaches Matthews, Mary's efficient administrative assistant, told me this story about the modern-day Good Samaritan:

As Mary and the young seminary student who lives with her family were leaving First Baptist Church after an evening service, they noticed a group of teenagers surrounding a young boy, who was lying in the street. Mary has an intense interest in young people, and she took a closer look. The seventeen-year-old boy barely weighed ninety-two pounds, and he had passed out. "He was so pitiful-looking," Mary said later as she described the youth.

It was learned the boy was a runaway from Houston, and had sought the comfort of the large downtown church. All he had were the clothes he wore and the small Bible given him by the church. That night he had received spiritual nourishment, but needed physical sustenance as well—he had not eaten all day.

Attempts were made to house him at the YMCA across the street, but there was no room available. A mission had housed him one night, but he couldn't go back because he lacked the funds to pay for additional nights.

Mary, who could have easily paid for the boy to stay at Dallas's finest hotel, instead took the boy to her beautiful home. She not only fed him, but, after he was bathed, gently tucked his tired body into a comfortable bed.

The next day Mary saw to it the boy was taken to her personal physician. There it was diagnosed that the rash on his frail body was from body lice. In addition, the doctor reported he had the worse case of malnutrition he had ever seen.

Because of the lice, the boy's clothes had to be burned and Mary's houseguest—a student at Criswell Bible Institute—learned a lesson in goodness by taking the boy to a department store and buying him an entire new wardrobe.

Goodness did not end with the boy being fed and clothed. Mary saw to it that he found a home at the Happy Hills Farm near Dallas when attempts to locate his mother failed. Mary has kept in touch by writing to the youngster as well as remembering him on his birthday.

Jesus made it clear that those who inherit his Kingdom will be those who show goodness: "For I was hungry, and you gave Me something to eat; I was thirsty, and you gave Me drink: I was a stranger, and you invited Me in; naked, and you clothed Me; I was sick, and you visited Me; I was in prison, and you came to Me." The bewildered righteous asked, "When did you do all of that?" and Jesus so lovingly answered, "To the extent that you did it to one of these brothers of Mine, even the least of them, you did it to Me." (Matt. 25:35–40).

Mary, the essence of goodness, says, "The more you give of your time and your talents, the more you are blessed in return." Mary never misses an opportunity to share her love for Jesus Christ to all with whom she comes in contact.

"When my last will and testament is read, no one will be surprised when it says, 'Being of sound mind I spent—and gave away—every last cent I had.'"

"You can never outgive the Lord," says Mary, who has laid up her treasures in heaven.

Dale Evans

FAITHFULNESS

The fruit of the Spirit is love,
joy, peace, patience, kindness, goodness,
FAITHFULNESS. . . .

Dale Evans

Commitments aren't hard to make—just hard to keep. Faithfulness is the property that flows from love and continues in love.

It is easy to give up when the going gets a little rough. But the characteristics Christ wants us to possess continue regardless of circumstances.

I once heard of a gentleman in London who watched a little three-year-old girl with a bright red coat and a tiny play shovel picking up one piece of coal at a time from the massive black ton left in the streets. Piece after piece she picked up, carrying each chunk to her house and down to the basement, carefully laying each one beside the furnace. Finally the gentleman couldn't contain himself any longer. "Little girl," he said, "you'll never get enough to warm you that way."

But the young child looked up innocently at the stranger and said, "Sir, I will if I work long enough."

Too often we wait for a big job to be dropped into our laps, and disdain the little everyday tasks we are asked to do. But nothing is small that is done for God. If David had never tackled the bear and the lion, he would not have been ready for Goliath. Our faithfulness in doing our appointed tasks is all Christ demands. Paul reminds us, "Be ye steadfast, unmovable, always abounding in the work of the Lord" (1 Cor. 15:58, KJV).

A woman in the kitchen spreading peanut butter on bread for her children is just as important—if that's where God wants her—as a missionary on the foreign field spreading the gospel to those who will listen. Billy Graham's wife, Ruth, has an appropriate motto hanging over her kitchen sink: "Divine service conducted here three times daily."

Unfaithfulness is a major factor in the breakup of so many marriages. The promise of "forever" sometimes seems as obsolete as the horse and buggy. Everyone readily agrees there is value in commitment, but often people struggle with the permanence that commitments are supposed to have. The wedding vows exhort the bridal couple to be "faithful unto death," but too often they play the charade of promising "forever" and meaning "for now."

One number-one example of faithfulness is Jesus Christ himself. He went about doing his Father's will, always remaining true to his principles and his commands. He was faithful to his Father, who sent him to die on the cross.

Daniel led an uncompromising life—one of unashamed boldness and unblemished faith. He was a unique man, and he never lowered the standards of his own relationship to God, whether he was talking to pagan kings or to peers. And his faithfulness to God gained him unmeasurable blessings; God raised him to a position of high influence.

The Hebrew word for faithfulness, *hesed*, refers to the dual motions of love and fidelity or steadfastness and tenderness. God's faithfulness is manifested in nature—the sun, moon, and stars; the beasts, the birds, and all living things are proof of the fact that once God spoke his word it has never been rescinded.

For Dale Evans, faithfulness to God was not an easy road. She didn't learn to be faithful until she learned she needed him more than he needed her.

Frances Octavia Smith entered the world October 31, 1912, in a tiny town in Texas. Being the first grandchild in the family, she never lacked attention. The youngster loved to sing, and her love of performing often got her into embarrassing situations. "I would break away from my parents when the lovely gospel music started in church, and I would dance down the aisle," she remembers.

An itinerant evangelist came to her church and presented the old, old story of Jesus and his love in such a dramatic way that the ten-year-old youngster reached out to Christ. "It was an honest response, but I was not ready to turn my whole life over to him," she says. The fun-loving girl was afraid that God might hold her back from doing something she wanted on her own.

Even though dancing was forbidden by her church, Dale talked her mother into chaperoning school dances, so that she could attend also. At age fourteen, she met her first steady boyfriend, and they went everywhere together. Soon they eloped.

The marriage was doomed for failure from the start, and lasted fewer than twelve years. But it produced a son, Tom, who would much later be the guiding force in bringing his mother into obedience to Jesus Christ.

A move to Memphis brought new friends, new activities, and once again church attendance. Still a teenager, Frances attended business school and then got a job as a secretary for an insurance firm.

Having more interest in singing than typing, the young lady grabbed at an opportunity to sing on a radio program. Frances Fox made her debut playing and singing "Mighty Lak a Rose." It wasn't long before civic organizations were asking her to sing at luncheons and banquets. Her first musical job with pay was in Louisville, Kentucky, and it was there the program director gave her her new name—Dale Evans. He picked it because it was impossible to mispronounce.

Her greatest goal was to make a name for herself, and she found singing jobs in Dallas and Chicago, working for dance bands and doing one-nighters in hotel ballrooms. Yet she was torn between her desire to be a good mother and her dream of making it big in show business.

One day she came home from work to find Tommy had severe pains in his arms and legs. It was a time when polio was crippling children across the country, and Dale prayed as she took the youngster to the hospital for a spinal tap. "Tearfully I promised God I would give him top priority if Tom's test would prove negative," Dale remembers. God kept his end of the bargain, and for a short time Dale kept hers by reading her Bible daily and praying. However, her musical ambition was much stronger than her spiritual devotion, and she soon forgot her promise to God.

Dale moved back again to Texas and the small community life, but she was determined not to let her parents support her and her son. She found a job singing in Dallas, and within a year she married a musician and they moved to Chicago.

Dale regularly took her son to church; she wanted him to have what she herself did not have—a firm relationship with Christ. At times the minister's sermons would be disturbing to Dale, and she would feel guilty about not taking a stand for Christ. She was afraid if she were faithful to him it might cost her something—something that might jeopardize her career. Part of her wanted to be a good wife and mother, part of her wanted to be a known entertainer—and she was not ready to fully commit herself to either.

Out of the blue she got an invitation to a screen test in Hollywood. Twentieth Century Fox offered her a one-year contract with pay of four hundred dollars a week. It was an offer she couldn't refuse.

The contract and the good income still left Dale with an emptiness and a lack of satisfaction. "We attended church every Sunday," she says, "but I always left my faith on the church steps after the service." Her son was growing into a wise and considerate Christian boy, but she conned herself into thinking that God would understand why she couldn't be faithful to her heavenly father. Someday when there was more time to give him, she could then devote her life to him.

Now Dale regrets that during the days of touring the army and air bases in Texas, she didn't make use of the opportunities to share a bit of spiritual hope with the boys.

But at last her career began to take off. She was under contract with Republic Studios and was cast in many pictures. Even though she had never thought about doing Westerns, she accepted the role of the Mexican girl opposite Roy Rogers in *The Cowboy and the Senorita*. Roy, a widower with three children, was not a typical Hollywood character, and his down-home personality was a refreshing breath of air to Dale.

Dale's marriage declined as she spent long waking hours on the set and her musician husband worked into the wee hours of the morning. In 1945 they were divorced.

World War II knocked a few jobs out of Dale's hands.

She entertained for the USO, doing around six hundred shows. Young Tommy was involved at the First Baptist Church of Hollywood, and occasionally would be accompanied by his mother. Even though sermons hit her squarely between the eyes, the career-minded woman refused to change her course.

Her picture with the King of the Cowboys was a success, and soon the studios were casting her in all the westerns opposite the famed Roy Rogers. Their friendship grew.

Between "takes" on the set, Roy and Dale spent a lot of time talking. One day the talk turned to religion. Dale declared her faith in Christ, but confessed that since she only had time for God on Sundays, she was not a 100-percent Christian. Roy listened, but when she asked if he took his children to Sunday school, his answer cut her down. Sunday was his day to rest. Besides, how could a loving God let helpless, innocent children be born with bad hearts or crippled legs? "If you can tell me how God can let those orphans and injured children suffer, then I would be interested in going to church. I've seen the people in our little church go down the aisle, but the rest of the week they would be back where they had always been. There was no difference in their lives."

Dale kept silent. She had walked that aisle herself, and she knew there wasn't much difference in *her* life.

A year later, as the nation's favorite cowboy and cowgirl participated in a rodeo, Roy asked Dale what her plans were for New Year's Eve. "I don't know," she replied. Just before riding off, the King of the Cowboys proposed, "Why don't we get married?"

On their wedding day, doubts began to crowd into Dale's mind, as she questioned whether another marriage was right for her. How could she handle three stepchildren?

She bowed her head and asked God to give her the strength.

Dale found being a stepmother extremely difficult. Roy's children resented her taking their mother's place. One day Tom suggested she take them to Sunday school. That Sunday Tom took the entire brood, but denies he conspired with the pastor on the sermon. The Holy Spirit was convicting Dale, and she squirmed through the entire service. That night, home in her room, she cried out to God on her knees, poured out her heart and asked his forgiveness. It was at this point Dale found out the real meaning of faithfulness.

When Roy returned home from a trip, she couldn't wait to share with him her exciting news of accepting Christ. "That's good for you, but don't go overboard," were Roy's words of caution to her. "And don't force it on me."

Dale started taking the children to church regularly, as well as reading her Bible and praying with the children at bedtime. She also asked Roy to go along to church, but never pushed him.

After one of the few arguments in their marriage, Dale retreated to the bedroom in tears. Roy stayed up late that night, thinking. The next morning, before Dale could ask, Roy announced he was going along to church. When the sermon was over and the invitation was given, Roy made his way down the aisle to accept Christ.

The doctors had told Dale she would never be able to bear another child. However, they were proven wrong when, on August 25, 1950, little Robin Elizabeth Rogers was born. Perhaps God was testing Dale's faithfulness in giving the Rogers a Mongoloid child to love. The new mother's heart cried out with a lot of questions to God but an inner voice calmly said, "Trust me, trust me." Dale learned to put her trust and faith in God, knowing he cared.

The doctors told the Rogers family all they could do for little Robin was to love her. As they poured out their love on her, they in turn noticed the family was drawing closer together. They knew Robin would not be with them long, but instead of dwelling on the negative they decided to enjoy the time she was with them.

Billy Graham invited Roy and Dale to share their testimony at his crusade in Houston. The only way they could make the trip was to fly rather than take the train as they usually did. Dale was afraid of flying, and had vowed never to fly while Robin was living for fear a crash would leave the little girl motherless. Struggling with her decision, she finally realized God wanted her to be at the crusade sharing with the thousands who would attend. There she could tell the people about the special qualities Robin had brought to their home—love and understanding. God richly blessed Dale for her faithfulness in flying to Houston.

Robin died shortly before her second birthday, and Dale decided to write a book to share Robin's story. After rejections from two publishers, Dale was about to give up, but Roy urged her to be patient. Finally, *Angel Unaware* was not only published, but also became a best-seller, with the proceeds going to the National Association for Retarded Children.

There was enough love in the Rogers' home to include even more children. During a visit to Hope Cottage in Dallas, Dale had fallen in love with a Choctaw Indian girl. Roy lost his heart to a handicapped little boy during intermission at one of his rodeos. When the cowboy and his wife arrived back home in Los Angeles, Dodie and Sandy had been added to the Rogers clan.

The "Roy Rogers and Dale Evans Show" was one of

the most popular TV shows during its run from 1951 through 1964. And although their public appearance schedule was full, Dale and Roy never missed an opportunity to share their message of Christian faith.

During this time the Rogers family continued to grow. Dr. Bob Pierce of World Vision, International, found a little Korean girl, renamed Debbie, to live with them. Marion, an orphan they met while touring Scotland, came to their home for a summer visit. There she sensed a warmth and love she had never received before, and insisted on staying longer.

The next nine years were happy, busy years for the Rogers' international family. Then, in 1964, tragedy struck. Twelve-year-old Debbie joined with her church youth group on a bus trip to take gifts to an orphanage in Mexico. Just after the bus left San Diego, it was involved in an accident, and Debbie was killed instantly. Nine years the youngster had been part of the fun-loving Rogers family. Now they grieved for her, but they had the assurance their daughter was in heaven. Again, Dale wrote a book—this time to tell Debbie's story. She donated the proceeds of *Dearest Debbie* to World Vision, which had made it possible for Debbie to be in the Rogers' household.

In 1965 the Rogers moved to Apple Valley in southern California. About this time Sandy, who was having difficulty in school, began urging Roy and Dale to sign for him to enlist in the army. He volunteered for Vietnam, but instead was sent to Germany. There he worked hard, and soon attained the rank of Pfc. One night, after twenty-six days of grueling maneuvers, his fellow soldiers urged him to celebrate his new rank by drinking hard liquor, and he took the challenge, wanting to be a man. But the drinking proved too much for him. He fell unconscious and died the next morning.

Heartbreak once again could have caused Dale to retreat. But she had learned the quality of God's faithfulness, and picked up the pieces. She told Sandy's story to the world in a book called *Salute to Sandy*.

Roy and Dale, who have become legends in the entertainment world, continue to spread their goodwill and peace around the globe. Whether it is on television shows, at charity benefits, on record albums, or in one of the eighteen books Dale has written, her faithfulness to God has been made known. She says with the Psalmist: "I will sing of the mercies of the Lord for ever: with my mouth will I make known thy faithfulness to all generations" (Ps. 89:1).

Joan Winmill Brown

GENTLENESS

The fruit of the Spirit is love, joy, peace, patience, kindness, goodness, faithfulness, GENTLENESS. . . .

Joan Winmill Brown

What do you think of when you think of gentleness? A butterfly? A lamb? Or perhaps a baby's kiss?

What man, in an attempt to visualize a god, would ever think of a *gentle* god? Most men would want power and strength associated with their god.

Yet the psalmist sings in his hymn of praise, "Thou hast also given me the shield of thy salvation: and thy right hand hath holden me up, and thy *gentleness* hath made me great" (Ps. 18:35, KJV, italics mine).

The rare passage of Scripture in which Jesus speaks of his own personality reads: "I am gentle and humble, and you shall find rest for your souls" (Matt. 11:29, TLB). Isaiah speaks of Jesus as one who would "gather the lambs with his arm, and carry them in his bosom, and shall gently lead those that are with young" (Isa. 40:11, KJV). And in the book of James we are told that "the wisdom that is from above is first pure, then peaceable, gentle, and easy to be entreated" (3:17, KJV).

These verses not only reveal aspects of God's nature, they also whisper of a need in people to be handled gently.

Apparently it is a need one never outgrows, regardless of how callous one appears to have become.

We live in a brutal world—a world in which the qualities of meekness and gentleness are often shunned. Perhaps that's because a thinking person realizes that living a life of gentleness requires more strength that he possesses. "This quality of life does not come from a position of feeble impotence, but rather from a tremendous inner strength and serenity. Only the strong, stable spirit can afford to be gentle," says Phillip Keller in his book, *A Gardener Looks at the Fruits of the Spirit.* Only the person filled with the resources of God himself can dare to be gentle. The Holy Spirit came to fill the believer's life. The fruit of the Holy Spirit are powerful testimonies to the truth of Christ's gospel.

The verse in Psalm 18 is echoed in 2 Samuel 22:36. "Thy gentleness hath made me great" (KJV). Another way of interpreting the words, "made great" in these verses is "increased." Under the harsh hand of a cruel world, the one who has found the gentleness of God and who is "made great" by it becomes the one who no longer fears granting the grace of gentleness to others. Such a person, increased by the very presence of God's Spirit within, has the resources to reach out tenderly and touch those who are hurting.

James speaks of tenderness succinctly: "The wisdom that comes from heaven is first of all pure and full of quiet gentleness. Then it is peace-loving and courteous. It allows discussion and is willing to yield to others; it is full of mercy and good deeds. It is wholehearted and straightforward and sincere. And those who are peacemakers will plant seeds of peace and reap a harvest of goodness" (3:17–18, TLB).

Shakespeare wrote, "He jests at scars, that never felt a

wound." Perhaps it is in being wounded that the human heart realizes the need for gentleness. Perhaps out of the school of pain comes the soul best prepared to reveal the fruit of gentleness.

Joan Winmill Brown is one thus schooled. Wounded as a child by the early and unexpected death of her mother, baby brother, and her close young cousin, Joan's need for gentleness was only partly met by her father's love. Shuttled from home to home while her father's traveling job kept him on the road most of the time, Joan's needs for security—for stability—were left unmet. She tasted the bitter dregs of life far too soon.

The tenderness of the headmistress at Joan's English girls' school made a deep impression on the lonely child. This woman's single explanation of the gospel of Jesus Christ planted seeds of hope in Joan's heart—seeds, however, that would not bring forth life until many dark years later.

Anxious to escape the pain and sadness of her own life, Joan became an actress, and soon was climbing the ladder of success on the London stage. She loved "always pretending to be someone else." What she didn't love, however, was having to cope with the stresses that constantly challenged her sensitive nature. She was acting both on and off stage—trying unsuccessfully to convince herself and others that such a life was the ultimate fulfillment. Eventually the struggle became too much for her; she tried to hide her fear and guilt in a haze of barbituates.

Finally, a nervous collapse revealed chasms of need in Joan's soul that the theatre—that life itself—could not fill. At a time when she was on the brink of suicide, she went to hear Billy Graham in London. There the words, "Come unto me, all ye that labor and are heavy laden, and I will give you rest," called Joan out of despair into light, and hope, and healing. Jesus drew Joan out of her downward spiral, and that night she yielded to the lordship of Christ.

Today, more than twenty-five years later, Joan lives in California with her husband, Bill. They have two sons.

Bill is perhaps more aware than anyone of the gentleness the Holy Spirit has brought forth in Joan. He says, "The nightmare of Joan's life before finding Christ accounts, no doubt, for the love and compassion she feels for anyone with an aching heart. So many people have told me that, to them, Joan is the most gentle person they know. A friend once remarked, 'I love to be around Joan. Her calm and gentle spirit makes me forget I have any problems.' "

Joan chuckles as she gives a quick, honest retort, "I might look calm and gentle—but they don't know what's going on inside." She continues, "Like other aspects of the Christian walk, seeking to be gentle is a daily experience. The *real* Joan Winmill Brown isn't so gentle. I pray each day that the *redeemed* Joan Winmill Brown is the one others will meet."

For the first fifteen years of their marriage, the Browns did not have a home of their own. Bill's work with Billy Graham required twenty-two moves by the time their first child was fourteen years of age. Inevitably, within weeks of the birth of each healthy, lively son, Joan was packing up to move again. To this woman—who was once warned by doctors never to "overdo"—God gave the grace to live an unsettled life, moving from city to city every few months.

David, her youngest son, now twenty years old, received the blessing of his mother's gentleness all through his childhood. "My mother's quiet discipline probably had a greater effect on me than the forceful correction my dad showed. I always appreciated the fact that my mom would never put me down in front of others. I was never embarrassed by her in front of my friends. If I did something wrong, in her own special way she would take me aside later and correct me. I listened, because I hated to hurt her."

Joan's other son, a burly twenty-three-year-old policeman, speaks proudly of his mother. "She has always been so very supportive in everything I wanted to do. She encouraged me so very much both when I became a paramedic and later a policeman.

"When I dated, I knew she was praying for me. Even when I dated a non-Christian, she didn't critize me—but just prayed harder, I suppose." When Bill, Jr. became engaged to his sweet Christian wife, Donna, Joan openly cried tears of thanksgiving, remembering the many times that, on her knees, she had prayed her son would meet just the right one.

David came home from school one day and said, "Do you know that of all my friends, I'm the only one with the original parents?" (Some were on the third and even the fourth father!) In an age when so many marriages are breaking up, the three men in Joan Brown's life would probably agree it is her gentle, understanding ways that have held theirs together. Bill, Sr. is the first to admit that his is a blunt, rather aggressive personality. "If Joan were like me," he says, "we would never have made it through twenty-five years of marriage."

But Joan's tenderness reaches far past the circumference of her home. In the nine years that I've worked as executive secretary for her husband, I've been able to observe her sensitivity, born of the wounds of confusion and emptiness she once felt outside of Christ. Joan is quick to respond to those who are in pain. From her there is never a harsh word; there is always a word of encouragement and an expression of interest in what the other person is feeling.

Her good friend Wanda Ross says, "Gentleness is

defined as a quality that is mild, amiable in nature and disposition, kind and patient, not harsh or abrupt but soft and refined.

"Joan is the epitome of gentleness. I sensed it years ago when we first met, before marriage and a family and the California hilltop home where she and Bill reach out to so many of us who are the recipients of their love and concern.

"But Joan's gentleness is far more than a personality trait with which one is naturally endowed. In the Psalms, David intuitively refers to the gentleness of God which made him great. It was a divine gift, one of the Father's essential qualities which elevated a shepherd lad to a throne of power and greatness.

"It is this superb kind of gentleness that characterizes Joan, producing that greatness which is the essence of a life wholly committed to the giver of every good and perfect gift."

Numbered among the host of friends Joan considers very special is a mother she comforted for months when a son was lost in the Vietnam war; a neighbor whose husband deserted her, and with whom Joan would meet to pray; Rose, a dope addict whose "roller coaster" experience with the Lord required months of counseling by Joan; and Jettee. Jettee is a black friend who does not have a living relative, but who, for over twenty years, has been part of Joan's family. Each Christmas the Browns carry no less than ten gifts to Jettee's small apartment, all beautifully wrapped with great quantities of love.

Another friend of Joan's is Pat. They first met when Joan visited a jail to share her testimony. Pat was wearing a shapeless prison dress and shoes that did not fit properly. She smoked a cigarette all the time Joan spoke. After speaking about the forgiveness that Christ could give, Joan asked them to pray with her. When she looked up, Pat was crying.

As the others left, Pat stayed behind. "There's no hope for me," she said, "I have failed God so terribly." When Joan turned to 1 John 1:9, Pat quickly said, "I know that verse—that won't help me."

Joan read the verse anyway, "If we confess our sins, he is faithful and just, and will forgive our sins and cleanse us from all unrighteousness" (KJV).

Joan pointed specifically to the word *all.* Pat took a long look at the passage in the Bible. Then she looked up into Joan's caring eyes and said, "I've never thought about that word *all.*" They prayed once more, and when Pat finished asking Christ into her life she looked up. Once again there were tears in her eyes. But these tears were happy tears now—she had reached out and grasped the hope the Savior offers.

Though scores of letters passed between them in the months that followed, Joan never asked Pat what her crime was. Joan never saw her as a criminal, but only as a person who, like herself, needed the cleansing that Christ alone can give.

As a new Christian, Pat finished serving the many remaining months of her sentence. After her release, she would often visit that very same jail to share her experiences with Christ—and especially the spirit of love that came to her first through Joan's gentle witness.

Joan Winmill Brown found the gentleness of God in Christ Jesus. His gentleness, as the Psalmist says, "has made her great"—has given her a heart big enough to see the world in pain around her and to touch it gently. And, because she has been wounded, Joan never laughs at scars.

Anne Ortlund

SELF-CONTROL

The fruit of the Spirit is love, joy,
peace, patience, kindness, goodness,
faithfulness, gentleness,
SELF-CONTROL.

Anne Ortlund

Human nature cries out to be disciplined. No matter how much social trends try to influence society with a lackadaisical, "let it all hang out" philosophy, people—young and old—still know that the self-controlled life is the happiest and the most fulfilled.

Young people, for instance, tired of the passé "hippie" lifestyle, have turned by the millions to the rigid, organized cults and religious sects. (In this quest to find identity, a good share of them, thank God, have turned to Jesus Christ.) Take a look at the discipline of "EST." During training seminars, devotees must sit in silence for hours, being told that "they are responsible for what they are." Sun Myung Moon, in spite of his rigid timetables and work assignments, has swept flocks of young people into his fold.

Not long ago, at an airport, I stood observing several followers of Hare Krishna. Like robots who had obviously been programed, they aggressively went about their job of approaching people about their religion or begging for money. "If only we Christians had that kind of zeal and discipline," I thought.

God left us with his Holy Spirit to direct us and to

bring our energies under control. He doesn't want us to just take life as it comes; he wants us to discipline ourselves in order to get where he wants us to be. Philippians 3:12–13 says, "I haven't learned all I should even yet, but I keep working toward that day when I will finally be all that Christ saved me for and wants me to be. . . . I am still not all I should be but I am bringing all my energies to bear on this one thing: Forgetting the past and looking forward to what lies ahead" (TLB).

Sometimes one undisciplined moment can ruin our day—we let our laundry pile up until there is nothing to wear or we yield to that piece of chocolate after dieting for weeks. But think how constantly devastated the *totally* undisciplined person is! For too many people the lack of self-control has become a way of life.

It doesn't have to be that way. If we could only realize early in life that we don't automatically inherit a lack of self-control! It comes by choice. And we are promised God's help as we learn to discipline ourselves: "Let God train you, for he is doing what any loving father does for his children. . . . Cheerfully submit to God's training so that we can begin really to live" (Heb. 12:7, 11, TLB).

Even though our days never seem long enough to accomplish the tasks before us, we must learn to organize and set goals for each day. Every day may be crowded with chores, but we must not lose sight of the really important things that are still going to matter when we are not so busy. This includes deepening our experience with God and bringing others to an acquaintance with him.

We are faced with decisions every day; in one way or another, we are constantly at a fork in the road. When we do make a wrong choice, it does no good to worry about our failures. Rather, it is important to learn to cope with such a situation. We must learn to pull ourselves together again and redouble our efforts as we move ahead.

The hallmark of a self-controlled, reliable person is not only the ability to do a job, but also the responsibility to complete the work when promised. One must always have a target in mind—although goals must of course be realistic. If you try to teach a child how to ride a bicycle, you can't expect him to immediately ride in a three-day bike race or steer his way through heavy traffic! Priorities must be set in planning a schedule and work should be done in specific small steps at a regular, steady pace. All too often people have too many interests, and they lack the discipline to follow through on the important activities.

The founder and chairman of the board of the large MacDonald's hamburger chain once said, "The longer I live, the more firmly convinced I become that the essential factor that lifts one man above his fellows in terms of achievement and success is his greater capacity for self-discipline. Talent plays a part, but talent and aptitude does not make the final difference."

After a great pianist gave an outstanding concert, he was introduced to an amateur who said, "I'd give anything in the world to be able to play like you." The pianist looked him in the eye and said, "No, you wouldn't." He remembered the sacrifices, the long hours of practice—the discipline it had taken to achieve his position of status. And he could perceive that the amateur was not willing to pay the price.

One of my favorite definitions of self-control is "the means by which the human being gains command of his abilities and uses them." William Barclay, the English theologian, said, "Self-control is the virtue which enables a person to master his own life so that he is able to be the servant of others."

When I think of those statements, I immediately think of Anne Ortlund—pastor's wife, mother, musician, author, lecturer, and yet a woman with enough time to disciple new Christians and care about her neighbors.

Anne laughed when I showed surprise that I had found her listed phone number in the directory. Here was the pastor's wife of the Lake Avenue Congregational Church (one of Los Angeles' largest)* and the successful author of *Disciplines of the Beautiful Woman,* which has sold over one hundred thousand copies, so easily accessible. "Availability—that's what it's all about," this busy woman told me.

Will power or self-control comes in varying degrees. Anne says, "Self discipline doesn't affect anybody but ourselves, because God deals with each Christian in his own way. We aren't cookie-cutter Christians all stamped out. It's easy for us when we get a vision of self-discipline to forget and start disciplining each other and being critical and wondering, 'why doesn't she do it this way, because it worked for me.' We cannot make rules for each other, but it is most important that we make laws for ourselves."

Anne grew up in a military family. "Father was a general in the army, but mother was also a 'general' in her own way," she says. "My parents came to know the Lord when I was six, and for the next forty years they taught Bible classes on all the army posts where they were stationed." Anne reminisces about her father and mother—how they would grow flowers and vegetables and on Saturdays take them to people who were sick or hurting. "Daddy was both tough and tender in his leadership—a velvet-covered brick," Anne remembers.

---

* Since this chapter was written, the Ortlunds have moved to Newport Beach, California, where Ray Ortlund is pastor of Mariners Church.

Even though the family moved about every two years, Anne fondly recalls her mother making the curtains in each new home fit as though they were going to be there a million years.

An early lesson in self-discipline began for Anne when, at the age of seven, she began piano lessons. Later, as soon as her feet could reach the pedals, she began organ lessons. Eventually, she became proficient enough to be an organ major in college, where she earned a Bachelor of Music degree. Now, for over a dozen years, Anne has been organist on the "The Joyful Sound" radio program.

Asked if she felt being a pastor's wife had pushed her further into the direction of exemplifying self-control, she admitted it probably had. But she feels she developed self-control out of pride: "Our first little church was in rural Pennsylvania, and Ray had just graduated from Princeton. We were both twenty-six, and we had three babies close together in age. There were eleven hundred people in that town and I noticed that everybody tried to race the others to get the wash out on the line on Monday mornings. This was status! I never won, but I soon became aware of what was expected of me.

"I feel that I am naturally lazy, but the Lord has never allowed me to have a lazy kind of lifestyle. Then too, pride kept me busy cleaning the house, whether I liked it or not. There was a constant stream of members from our congregation walking in the front door."

Self-control has become a way of life for Anne, and she is convinced that the Holy Spirit has had a part in pushing her along. In those early years of her marriage, she got into a routine of changing diapers, washing bottles, and soothing pleading cries. One day she realized she had gone for months without a quiet time. "I got so ornery and so hard to live with. I could see the hurt look on Ray's face when I snapped at him," she said. "Fortunately, I got desperate enough to want to spend time alone with God." Since Anne is normally a sound sleeper, she made a pact with the Lord that, if he would wake her, she would meet him from two until three in the morning. The young mother kept her promise until her family demands lightened. And she never regretted the missed sleep.

There were areas of self-control that took longer for Anne to learn. She confessed that her own tongue has been an area of grief to her. "Ever since I was a little girl I used to exaggerate. I don't know why. I would start with the truth and just go from there. I guess I just had a flair for the dramatic. If a story sounded good with four people at the scene, it probably would sound better if there were six. But as I began to mature in the Holy Spirit, I was pricked by this tendency. A few years ago, I really got serious about that sin in my life and began to call it 'lying.'

"The Lord was dealing with me about that. One time we were having a sharing time at our church, and here was I, the pastor's wife, standing up before a thousand people, telling them I had no victory in my life about this problem. About ten months later, a dear young woman came to me and said, 'Anne, I've been meaning to ask you, how are you doing with your tongue? I've been praying for you ever since you mentioned that.'

"I had really felt the Lord was teaching me temperance with my tongue, but I hadn't realized the whole reason why. His results were twofold: Kathy Podley had disciplined herself to pray for me every single day, and through that God had poured strength into me. Discipline in the body of Christ strengthens each other."

If we are to master self-control, we must first learn that we are competing with no one but ourselves. A task that takes someone else an hour might take me three. This doesn't mean the other person is a genius and I'm incompetent—only that we work with different rhythms and at different paces.

I realized Anne certainly reflected self-control when I understood how she wrote her best-selling book, *Disciplines of the Beautiful Woman*. After spending more than a year gathering material and doing research, writing bits and pieces as sudden inspiration hit, Anne then took all of her material to a quiet spot to write—Hawaii.

"I have to work in total confinement. Maybe other people can sit down and write two or three hours a day and then go on to other things," she says, "but once I get a book in my head I have to spend all my time on that until it is done. I write very fast. *Disciplines of the Beautiful Woman* took six days a week for four weeks—twenty-four days. I simply started writing after breakfast and wrote until dinnertime, and on the seventh day I spent the time with my husband and son."

So each day, while Anne's husband, Ray, and son, Nels, enjoyed the sun, sand, and surf of Hawaii, she faithfully confined herself to writing *Disciplines of the Beautiful Woman*. That's real self-control!

Anne relates an experience that occurred after she had finished a talk at Wheaton College: "A young girl came up to me and said, 'I have given my life to Christ, and surrendered my heart to him. You mentioned we need to make fresh surrenders, and I did that—eighteen months ago.' The girl went on to say that everything had been wonderful for a few days, but that then she had seemed to slip back into the same old person she had always been.

"Right at that time there was a sanitation workers' strike in New York, and the newspapers had pictures of all the garbage piled up. So I said to that young woman, 'It's not something we do once and for all. Surrendering your life to the Lord is like taking out the trash. You do it day by day, moment by moment, hour by hour. We constantly need forgiveness and cleansing from our sin. If the last time you did that was eighteen months ago, you have eighteen months of accumulation to get rid of." Anne was able to point out to that young lady the importance of having Jesus fill our lives with those things that please him.

Self-control is a valuable virtue. Proverbs 16:32 says, "It is better to have self-control than to control an army" (TLB). Discipline is a totally personal thing between us and the Lord. In 1 Corinthians 9:24–27, Paul talks about the runner who must deny himself many things that would keep him from doing his best. Verse 26 says, "So I run straight to the goal with purpose in every step. I fight to win. I'm not just shadow-boxing or playing around." Verse 27 continues: "Like an athlete I punish my body, treating it roughly, training it to do what it should, not what it wants to. Otherwise I fear that after enlisting others for the race, I myself might be declared unfit and ordered to stand aside."

Notice Paul says *I* run, *I* fight, *I* punish my body, but he also makes it clear it's not a matter of putting ourselves together in our own strength, but his. God is the author of orderliness—not of confusion. He makes the planets go in their courses without bumping into each other. He does everything decently and in order.

When I asked Anne what she felt to be the most difficult areas of self-control, she quoted her pastor/husband. Ray Ortlund says the greatest temptations to every Christian are the easy chair, credit cards, banana cream pie, and television.

Anne disclosed that she is not a natural athlete. But her husband is physically active, and he has encouraged her to exercise. She has a daily routine of running up and down the stairs to help keep her trim figure. "I think everyone needs a moderate amount of exercise without being a nut. We can go overboard, and a body-beautiful consciousness can be another form of worldliness.

"One of the ways we can grieve the Holy Spirit is to become too occupied with ourselves," Anne said. "We can become fanatics and go all out on health fads." But the petite minister's wife believes the best diet is three sensible meals a day.

For many people the responsibility of managing money takes a lot of self-control. "We are tempted in our minds to covet. That's a violation of God wanting us to be content. The have-nots can be as materialistic-minded as the haves. Who knows the proportion of what they give to what they have? It's a relative thing. Each person has to decide for himself whether God would have him spend the money or not, and then God disciplines that particular heart," Anne says.

The woman described in Proverbs 31 certainly had the virtue of self-control: "She gets up before dawn to prepare breakfast for her household, and plans the day's work for her servant girls. She goes out to inspect a field, and buys it; with her own hands she plants a vineyard. She is energetic, a hard worker, and watches for bargains. She works far into the night! She sews for the poor, and generously gives to the needy. She has no fear of winter for her household, for she has made warm clothes for all of them. She also upholsters with finest tapestry; her own clothing is beautifully made—a purple gown of pure linen. . . . She watches carefully all that goes on throughout her household, and is never lazy. . . . Charm can be deceptive and beauty doesn't last, but a woman who fears and reverences God shall be greatly praised" (vv. 15–22, 27, 30, TLB).

Anne Ortlund

Anne writes in *Disciplines of the Beautiful Woman*, "Once I was studying Proverbs 31, the description of a 'worthy woman,' and it struck me in a new light. I noticed that twenty-two verses describe this woman's kindness, godliness, hard work, loving relationships—and only one verse out of the twenty-two describes how she looked. But she looked simply great! Verse twenty-two says, 'She makes coverings for herself; her clothing is fine linen and purple.' Purple was the fabric of the wealthy.

"Seeing this kind of proportion in Proverbs 31—one verse out of twenty-two describes her good looks—I prayed, 'Father, I want to give $\frac{1}{22}$ of my time to making myself as outwardly beautiful as I can; and I want to give all the rest of my time, $2\frac{1}{22}$ of my life, to becoming wise, kind, godly, hard-working, and the rest.' "

A Christian woman's appearance should always reflect self-control. Her clothing should enhance her but not consume her. Who you are is much more important than what you are wearing. Clothes need not be expensive to be attractive. Neatness, however, is vital to everyone's look. Never hang a dress in your closet with the hem falling out, but use self-discipline and fix it the minute you notice it. Then you'll never be frustrated when you are getting ready to go out and take that dress from a hanger.

Too many people lack self-control in spending time wisely. According to Anne, watching hour after hour of television can be a symptom of not finding our own life exciting enough. Our goals and ambitions must be set high enough to keep us stimulated. Friends should turn us on to stimulating conversation. Television is not the only means of using our time unwisely. Some people get lost in novels and read and read. Other people seem to spin their wheels by constantly doing and going, yet never seem to improve themselves or those around them. It's important that we question ourselves and make sure we are all he wants us to be.

As pressures and responsibilities began to crowd Anne's life, she saw the only way out was to have a notebook and live by it. "I'm still not organized, but my notebook is," she confesses. She carries it with her everywhere she goes, and keeps it handy at her nightstand in case she wakes up during the night and wants to jot down a thought.

Anne's brown notebook ("I like brown and it coordinates with what I wear," Anne told me) is divided into sections: "Not everyone will have need for the same sections I have, but mine can be guidelines for others."

The first section is the calendar section. She does her planning up to three months ahead, keeping a separate calendar page in her notebook for each day. On these pages, Anne writes down whatever she has to do. It might be shopping, calling the exterminator, keeping an appointment with someone, or relaying a message. As each project is finished, she draws a line through it. Then, after each day passes, she throws the page for that day away. If something has not been done, Anne jots it down for another day.

With this method, Anne is always able to look ahead to what is happening. She can avoid surprises and pace herself according to what is in store. She blocks out a week in November to address Christmas cards and another week to do Christmas shopping.

Another section of Anne's notebook is marked "Goals." In this section, Anne writes down both her lifetime and her short-term objectives. One of her lifelong goals is to leave a lasting mark on those around her; this she is doing by teaching her children godliness, disciplining other women, sharing her experiences in books, and writing hymns.

Anne also sets specific goals for each year. ("Goals should be measurable," she says.) This year one of her goals is to win six people to Jesus Christ, six to church membership, six to attend morning church service, and six to evening church. When she is flipping through her notebook, she checks her goals. It is then easy for her to evaluate her progress.

One section in her little brown book includes Bible study material. She reads the Bible through each year, taking notes. She also remembers portions by writing down meaningful passages. In addition, she keeps sermon notes; these she finds especially helpful in teaching others.

"Discipling" is another section—and this includes her lifetime goal of discipling one hundred women by the time she is seventy-five. She writes the names of the women she is discipling, along with their husbands' names, birthdays, prayer requests, the dates they meet, and what they have learned.

Writing down her prayers has been a revealing experience for the minister's wife. In still another section of her notebook, she expresses her joys, her needs, and her sorrows—the times she is happy and the times she is blue. Anne says it has been exciting to look back over the prayers in her notebook and see how God has answered them, even when she is unaware of it.

Anne Ortlund believes firmly that her notebook has kept her organized and within the bounds of self-control. It has been a tool of the Holy Spirit to grow the fruit of self-control in her life. And she has passed it on to others. Through the example of her life, and through her books and seminars, she has shared with hundreds of women what she has learned about discipline, about keeping her life in order and making daily decisions in the light of eternal values.